Praise For

"Jim Roddy's inspiration~~~~~~~~~~~~~~~~~~~~~ : for any executive with hiring responsibilities. You can start your journey to building the strongest team possible by reading this book."

Pat Williams
Senior Vice President of the Orlando Magic
Author of *Leadership Excellence*

"This book is spot on. I highly recommend *Hire Like You Just Beat Cancer* and have added the book to my success library. Jim Roddy's insight into the technical nature of hiring forces a discipline on managers with hiring responsibility to move beyond the shortcut we call *gut instinct*. Jim also crystallizes the point that hiring the best people who also fit into the company culture are not mutually exclusive goals; they are essential to hiring and retaining employees for the long term."

Steve Cuntz
President, BlueStar

"Jim Roddy's book *Hire Like You Just Beat Cancer* is a practical, humanistic approach to hiring and building a dynamic and dedicated workforce. Jim's perspective on the work/life balance is something most business books miss and can only be written by someone who has traveled the difficult and torturous path of cancer. This is a 5-star book that you won't want to miss."

Jeff Yelton
former President, ScanSource POS & Barcoding

"If you are responsible for hiring within your company, this is a must-read! If you are an executive that is responsible for hiring a hiring manager, this is a must-read. It contains tons of practical information. The probing questions during an interview in this book are a huge value in the hiring process all by themselves. Over the years, our company has used a lot of what is documented in this book. It works!"

Dean Crotty
President, North Country Business Products

"Roddy speaks about the importance of hiring people with good character traits. I loved his list of 18 character points and will use them in my future hiring decisions."

Jim Estill
Partner, Canrock Ventures
Founding Director of RIM

"Finally! Everything you have ever needed to know about hiring, all in a single book. Our management team has been accumulating Jim Roddy's HR materials from sessions at our industry association meetings, and now we can toss out all those unwieldy, tattered, and well-worn notes. But it is more than just a book on hiring. It is a philosophy on how to create sustainable corporate culture where excellence reigns and the bench is always filled with top talent."

Brad Holaway
President, Copperstate Restaurant Technologies

"I found *Hire Like You Just Beat Cancer* to be a wonderful resource for anyone who wants to hire 'smart.' It packs a lot of good info – tips, techniques, and best practices. It's a blueprint for hiring the best, then treating them right. I highly recommend it."

Sharon Armstrong
Author of *The Essential Performance Review Handbook, Stress-free Performance Appraisals, and The Essential HR Handbook*

"This book should be required reading for everyone who has responsibility for hiring. If you do not have a process for hiring top-tier talent, then implement these processes quickly. If you already have a policy, do your company a huge favor by comparing your interview process to Jim's recommendations. Once you have implemented Jim's policies or adjusted yours to follow his recommendations, your company's employee productivity will increase greatly."

David Callahan
Global Account Manager, Dell

"*Hire Like You Just Beat Cancer* is a must-read for anyone responsible for hiring and managing people. Regardless of your experience, you can learn from Jim Roddy's advice and proven strategies for recruiting, interviewing, and assembling a great team. Jim's personal story also entertains and inspires!"

Matt Bresee
President, Erie Bayhawks – members of the NBA Development League

"Jim Roddy is passionate about improving organizational effectiveness and profitability. He takes the subjective and complex process of hiring and reduces it to a *must-read* set of objective and manageable steps that will enhance any leader's ability to make better hiring decisions."

Mark Olson
President, APG Cash Drawer

"*Hire Like You Just Beat Cancer* should be mandatory training material for every hiring manager. Most hiring managers would balk at the idea of investing the time Jameson Publishing puts into the interview process, but the return on investment will be exponential and long-lasting. This book spells out how to identify the exceptional employees every company needs."

Trevor Brooks
Pre-Employment Services Consultant, ADP

"With *Hire Like You Just Beat Cancer*, Jim has provided a compelling set of hiring best practices with a long list of relevant examples and pragmatic interview resources and tools. Jim's plain-spoken writing style and openness in sharing candidate profiles, hiring successes and failures, and even his personal triumph over cancer all come together into a valuable resource that I will use to build better teams and hiring managers for the rest of my career."

Jeff Riley
CEO, Dinerware

"*Hire Like You Just Beat Cancer* is a must-have for anyone who ever conducts an interview. Jim Roddy provides details of his experiences in the hiring process, and it is experience which is the best way to learn. I continue to reference it before every interview."

Jason Cowan
President, Cowan's Retail Systems

"*Hire Like You Just Beat Cancer* reinvigorated my dedication to the hiring process and my excitement around getting the best person in the position. Jim Roddy's use of storytelling allows the reader to easily connect to the points being made. Hiring and retaining quality associates is something every business manager faces, and this book provides a quality playbook to solving this very real problem. The combination of strong advice plus Jim's entertaining presentation makes this book an interesting read. This book is relevant for companies of all sizes and for all levels of hiring."

Justin Scopaz
Vice President and General Manager, Ingram Micro Data Capture/POS Division

"This book is a real-world reminder of the trials that people face and how they affect businesses every day. This inspirational story will help you make better and more effective hiring decisions each and every time."

Will Atkinson
President, CAP Software

"Jim's commentary and ideas will provide you with the reasons for hiring the right employees for your team and provide you with some great ideas to help you bring the best people into your organization. This book is a must-read if you want to hire employees who make your business world-class."

Joe Finizio
President & CEO, Retail Solutions Providers Association

"In *Hire Like You Just Beat Cancer*, Jim Roddy blends wisdom and experience with humor while he walks you through the battle to hire the best fit for your job and your company. His focus on the behavioral style of interviewing and all of the great examples will help hiring managers focus on what's really important when making hiring decisions."

Stella LaPaglia, SPHR
AVP/HR Manager

"One of the biggest struggles in business today is building the right mix of individuals and getting them to function as a team. Jim Roddy sheds light on how to approach hiring effectively and get the best results."

John Giles
President/CEO, Future POS

"A textbook of interviewing. We spend more time with our co-workers every day than we do our spouse, yet only spend an hour or so getting to know if we want to spend our workday with these new employees. *Hire Like You Just Beat Cancer* is a thought-provoking tool to change your hiring practices for the improvement of your business and bring on new team members that will fit your company culture. We just used many of the ideas in this book for a recent hire and feel more secure about our latest decision than most past hires."

Dale Seefeldt
President, Tulsa Cash Register

"Nothing drives success of a business better than a dedicated team of qualified, driven individuals. In his book *Hire Like You Just Beat Cancer*, Jim Roddy gives priceless guidance on how to identify, recruit, and retain the best talent to help your company achieve and exceed its goals."

David Gosman
CEO, PC America
CEO, SNAP Services

"Jim Roddy does not want to waste time given a full cancer recovery. He applies this pragmatic intensity to this very real and down-to-earth book on hiring tips. The book offers hiring managers and HR professionals specific words to use and actions to take to get the filter and hire the right person. The book is pragmatic, experience-based, and relevant."

Dave Ulrich
Professor, Ross School of Business, University of Michigan
Partner, The RBL Group

HIRE
LIKE YOU JUST
BEAT CANCER

Hiring lessons, interview best practices,
and recruiting strategies for managers from a
cancer-surviving executive

JIM RODDY

www.JamesonPublishing.com

www.HowlandPeterson.com

© 2012 Jameson Publishing & Howland Peterson Consulting
All Rights Reserved.

First published by Dog Ear Publishing
4010 W. 86th Street, Ste H
Indianapolis, IN 46268
www.dogearpublishing.net

ISBN: 978-1-4575-1213-1

This book is printed on acid-free paper.

Printed in the United States of America

A portion of the proceeds from sales of
Hire Like You Just Beat Cancer will be donated to:

The Kanzius Cancer Research Foundation
(www.KanziusCancerResearch.com)
and
The American Cancer Society through Coaches vs. Cancer
(www.cancer.org.)

To order more copies of this book, go to:
www.HireLikeYouJustBeatCancer.com

On The Cover (left to right): Jameson Publishing employees Ed Hess, Sarah Howland, Tim Maciulewicz, Jon Dudenhoeffer, author Jim Roddy, Tracy Tasker, Tim Ulrich, Jenell Skemp, and Mike Suleski.

Special Thanks:
Editor — Maureen Haggerty
Proofreader — Paul DeSante
Photographer — Tim Rohrbach (www.RohrbachPhoto.com)

Hire Like You Just Beat Cancer is dedicated to:

My wife Barbara and our daughter Evelyn
I'm blessed by you every day. You have made me the world's
luckiest husband and daddy.

My mother Jacquelyn Roddy
Your passion for the English language and for caring about
others influences everything I do.

Jameson Publishing owners Rick and Terry Peterson
Thanks for your wisdom, your perseverance, and for your commitment
to building an organization with high-character people.

And this book is dedicated to anyone who ever beat cancer.

Contents

Introduction 1

Guaranteed-to-Not-Overwhelm-You Glossary 5

Part I – Guiding Principles for Hiring

1. The Importance of Accurate People Decisions................................9

2. Hire for "Bench Strength," Not Just for the Job at Hand 13

3. What to Look for During the Interview 19

4. Behavior-Focused Interviewing 27

5. Emotional Outcomes...35

6. Hiring Rules of Thumb 41

Part II – Decision-Making & Communication Skills

7. Decision-Making Skills 55

8. Communication Skills 63

Part III – Actionable Information

9. Effective Recruiting Tactics 77

10. Proven Pre-Employment Process 87

11. Uncovering, Exposing, & Overcoming Aversions.......................93

12. General Interview Best Practices Policies & Procedures 103

13. The Dinner Interview 109

14. The Final Aversions Interview 117

Part IV – 258 Tremendous Interview Questions 125

Final Words...161

Next Steps 163

About The Author 165

Introduction

Why title a book *Hire Like You Just Beat Cancer*? I'll give you the short version of my story:

- From 1993 to 1998, I was a self-employed sole proprietor, publishing a monthly magazine about high school, college, and minor league pro sports in northwestern Pennsylvania. It was called *SportsLook*. I'm certain you never heard of it.
- In 1998, harried by self-employment stresses such as 70-hour workweeks and the inability to afford anything other than SpaghettiOs for dinner, I took a real job as managing editor for Jameson Publishing. A publisher of national IT trade magazines and websites, Jameson is headquartered in my hometown of Erie, Pennsylvania.
- Since I had success with hiring on the editorial and production side of our business, the owners asked me to help interview and hire sales employees. After a couple sales candidates asked, "Why am I talking with an editor?" the owners changed my title to operations manager. It lacked the fanfare you see in the movies when someone is promoted, but it was a move up.
- Then I got cancer.

I was only 32 years old. I had to tell my teenage brother that if surgery showed that my colon cancer had spread to other organs, I might not be around through the end of his basketball season. As you can imagine, we were both scared and shared a long cry.

I also had to tell my boss and co-workers that even if things went well, I was going to be out of commission for two months after surgery. And, due to chemotherapy treatments, I would work only part time for most of the next year. If things didn't go well, the team would move on without me.

Before my diagnosis, I'd thought I understood the importance of hiring top-notch people. But it took being forced to step away from my co-workers for an extended period of time (with one of the options being stepping away *forever*) for me to realize that the people you hire truly make or break your business. It doesn't matter if you have the best product, best systems, best location, or a spotless reputation. Your situation will change eventually. When that happens, who's going to make the right adjustments to your business? Your people.

I hope you achieve two primary outcomes by reading this book.

1. I hope that, like me, you realize the people you hire will make or break your business. (But, unlike me, I don't want you to have to get cancer to learn that lesson.)
2. I hope you learn time-proven principles and techniques that will help you hire world-class co-workers.

At Jameson Publishing, where I'm now company president, we've made sure that every hiring manager understands those two lessons. Our company principles, which are posted on seemingly every wall in our headquarters and satellite offices, talk loudly about how to "Establish A World-Class Organization":

1. Employ only the best.
    a. Attract, hire, and retain quality employees who can build the company better than our current best.
    b. Pay higher-than-market salaries and bonuses on top of that.
    c. Incentivize to make employees feel the way the company feels.
    d. "Install managers who are among the ablest, most earnest, and reliable in the field of business." – J.D. Rockefeller

2. Build a reserve of capable employees who can move up to fill positions created by growth.
    a. Have at all times at least one subordinate with the ambition, people skills, technical competence, and values who could take over your position today.
    b. Cause managers to hire bench strength even for their star performers and for themselves.
        i. Offer jobs only to applicants you believe can grow beyond their starting position with us. To do otherwise runs the risk of not having enough capable employees to fuel our growth.

ii. Offer jobs to applicants capable of solving all the problems they'll encounter. We're flunking if it requires the department head to solve the department's problems.

c. Make room for capable employees who could grow into department heads or division presidents, so we don't lose them.

3. "Build a force of enthusiastic, loyal, harmonious co-workers." – Harvey Firestone

In *Hire Like You Just Beat Cancer*, you'll see short, easy-to-digest chapters filled with detailed examples and principles your business can adopt. You'll read about time-tested best practices your organization can implement immediately. If you do, I'm certain your business will improve. I know it's worked for us at Jameson. We're not the biggest business-to-business publisher in North America, but I'd put the quality of our employees up against those of any other publisher.

For example, our employees did a phenomenal job during the Great Recession of 2008. They understood the need to do more with less. To stay in business, we were forced to lay off several employees. And the ones who stayed took a hit financially. Operations employees went for more than two years without pay raises. Managers lost their overtime pay. With our revenue off nearly 33%, the take-home pay of most sales employees dropped by $10,000–$40,000. On top of that, for the first time in company history, we stopped our dollar-for-dollar 401(k) match. For 1 year, 11 months, and 9 days. (Yes, I was counting.) You'd think employees wouldn't have been able to work with all the complaining going on around them. But that's not what happened.

Our employees didn't complain, and they didn't just hold down the fort. They innovated and positioned each of our products to take advantage of growing sectors in their industries. In 2010, we grew our sales 20%, enabling us to turn on manager overtime pay and our 401(k) match. We began hiring again, because we had more customers to take care of. It was a monumental accomplishment in a tumultuous time. Our customers love our employees, and so do I.

Before we get on with the meat of this book, I should let you know that I've been cancer-free since 2002. I try to not think much about cancer, and I won't dwell on cancer throughout this book. But the lessons I learned when cancer knocked me down helped build me up as a hiring manager, and I apply those lessons aggressively every time we interview a potential employee.

Guaranteed-to-Not-Overwhelm-You Glossary

One of my biggest frustrations with other hiring systems is they require you to learn not only a new system, but a new language. *Hire Like You Just Beat Cancer* strives to use common business-world language and avoid hiring jargon. There are only a few terms in the book you might not be familiar with:

Aversion: A reason the job and your company might not be a good fit for the candidate. You will have aversions about every candidate, and every candidate should have aversions about you.

Character Traits: I'll define these in detail later, but want to share with you now the list of character traits we examine when assessing a candidate: prudence, justice, fortitude, temperance, ambition, work ethic, perseverance, honesty, kindness, responsibility, service, ongoing education, enthusiasm, humility, respectfulness, gratitude, loyalty, and generosity.

Hiring Manager: The person who interviews, hires, and eventually manages the candidate. The hiring manager doesn't need to be involved in every interview but, at a minimum, participates in the final stages of your hiring process.

Mapping: Does the candidate have the psychological makeup to be *inclined* to perform the activities of your job consistently, independently, and above your company standard? Or do you have to relentlessly push the candidate to perform the activity? For example, a sales candidate who has the skills to influence company presidents but finds that activity causes emotional anguish will not perform that activity consistently and is unlikely to succeed at the job.

One-for-One Test: This test requires candidates to do exactly what you want them to once they are hired. For example, if you're hiring a salesperson, set up a mock sales call in which the candidate tries to sell you something.

PART I

Guiding Principles for Hiring

CHAPTER 1

The Importance of Accurate People Decisions

Let's start with two of my favorite passages related to people decisions. The first is a lengthy quote from renowned business management author Peter Drucker. Please don't just read it; *absorb* it:

"People decisions are the ultimate — perhaps the only — control of an organization. People determine the performance capacity of an organization. No organization can do better than the people it has. The yield from the human resource really determines the organization's performance.

"And that's decided by the basic people decisions: who we hire and who we fire, where we place people, and who we promote. The quality of these human decisions largely determines whether the organization is being run seriously, whether its mission, its values, and its objectives are real and meaningful to people, rather than just public relations and rhetoric.

"Any executive who starts out believing that he or she is a good judge of people is going to end up making the worst decisions. To be a judge of people is not a power given to mere mortals. Those who have a batting average of almost a thousand in such decisions start out with a very simple premise: that they are not judges of people. They start out with a commitment to a diagnostic process.

"An executive has to learn not to depend on insight and knowledge of people but on a mundane, boring, and conscientious step-by-step process. Don't hire people based on your instincts. Have a process in place to research and test candidates thoroughly."

Now here's an excerpt from a 2006 Inc. Magazine article titled "The New Science of Hiring." Inc. talked with Dan Weinfurter, manager of a human resources consulting firm. Weinfurter estimates that he invests up to four weeks, plus his workers' billable hours, per interview. But he estimates that hiring a bad consultant could cost his company millions of dollars in salary, missed sales, and lost clients. **"I think the hiring process is the most important process in business," he says, "but it's probably the least disciplined in terms of how it's executed across American business."**

Here are those bold quotes again (unbolded, to save ink):
- "An executive has to learn not to depend on insight and knowledge of people but on a mundane, boring, and conscientious step-by-step process."
- "I think the hiring process is the most important process in business, but it's probably the least disciplined in terms of how it's executed across American business."

What Drucker and Weinfurter are saying isn't sexy. No one will make a movie about it. They're talking about common, unspectacular, block-and-tackle business best practices. Consistently great companies aren't built upon one whiz-bang idea. Their growth is based on a proven interview methodology that distinguishes great performers from average ones during the pre-employment process.

Before we talk in detail about hiring methodology, I want to make it clear that this book won't transform you into some sort of clairvoyant. Our methodology is going to be way less enchanting. But it will work.

When you offer someone a job, visualize yourself betting a sack of your company's money that your new hire will be successfully working with your company in 10 years. If every one of your new hires does not meet those criteria, you lose.

- Tenured, committed employees build companies and lead them to new opportunities. If a new hire remains with your company a few years or less, you suffer wasted training time and experience the harm of opportunity lost.

- You bet your money and your future with every job offer. Betting is about probabilities and odds. So don't bet against the odds.

- That said, all hires are risky, and a calculated gamble is sometimes warranted. The real damage to your company occurs if a new hire remains on your payroll for months (or years) without consistently demonstrating superior (or even satisfactory) performance. Make sure you have an efficient plan for getting new hires good or getting them gone.

At one particular Jameson Steering Committee meeting, we asked why one department consistently achieved outcomes while another regularly fell short. We identified two primary, intersecting reasons: our company culture and the people we hire.

If your stronger people — or a majority of your people — are committed to high quality and understand how to attain it, you'll achieve the outcomes you want. They'll surround underperformers and get them good or get them gone. Hire people *who have it in their DNA* to do the job. A sales rep with call reluctance is not going to make sales or be enthused at the long-term prospect of making calls. You're better off hiring someone with less-impressive skills who's excited about making calls because making calls will be in that employee's DNA even when your back is turned. Even if you share volumes of sales training manuals with the wrong hire, you're likely to miss your targets. We've learned that the core of a successful department is hiring the right people, then training them up.

The Wall Street Journal interviewed Barry Salzberg, global chief executive of professional services organization Deloitte Touche Tohmatsu, who emphasized the importance of finding a candidate who fits your organization. "The one thing that's most important is to be sure there is a very good marriage," Salzberg said. "This isn't about Deloitte just believing that the person we are interviewing is perfect for some role. It's also that person believing that Deloitte is perfect for the environment that they want to be in. I'm searching to determine whether that marriage is there. It shouldn't be one-sided, because if it is, it's not going to be a successful marriage. So I'm looking for values. I'm looking for priorities. I'm looking for a fit."

Hiring decisions are important, but don't fear making a hiring mistake so much that you become gun-shy and don't hire anyone. There's no substitute for experience and learning from your mistakes. The only way to learn is to get some scars. My company's best hiring managers have scars from past failed hires. If we ever meet in person, I'll show you my scars. If you want.

To reduce your chance of hiring errors, have a more experienced hiring manager validate your conclusions and suggest questions that could enhance your understanding of the situation. If you're so afraid of hiring the wrong person that you hesitate to hire *anybody*, you will not achieve your staffing goals. And your company will not achieve its growth goals.

CHAPTER 2

Hire for "Bench Strength," Not Just for the Job at Hand

"If each of us hires people who are smaller than we are, we shall become a company of dwarfs. But if each of us hires people who are bigger than we are, we shall become a company of giants."

– famed advertising executive David Ogilvy

When you're hiring for a salesperson, don't hire a salesperson. When you're hiring an entry-level manager, don't hire an entry-level manager. When you're hiring a receptionist, don't hire a receptionist. Kinda contradictory, eh?

Instead, hire someone who will start as a salesperson and could grow into a sales manager, sales trainer, or more. Hire someone who will be a fine entry-level manager, then grow into a division leader, vice president, or more. And hire a receptionist with the potential to maybe someday fill the role of company president. It's happened before.

Too often, we hire people whose full potential and ambition are invested in performing the jobs they're hired for. Then, when we need more from them, they're not able or willing to go the extra mile.

Your goal should be to have at all times (or be working toward) at least one employee with the skills, personality, character, mapping, ambition, and technical competence to take over your position right away. Without this:

1. If an opportunity for you to be promoted arises, you could be over-looked because no one else in your company is capable of doing your current job.
2. Your company will be unable to attain its growth goals quickly, reducing future profits and opportunities for your co-workers to achieve their career goals.
3. If you are incapacitated for a couple months or longer, the business could be damaged.

I learned that third lesson the hard way when I was diagnosed with cancer. But I was fortunate that we had hired several high-potential people who filled in for me when I was sidelined by my surgery and chemo treatments.

To illustrate the importance of hiring for bench strength, I'll offer several examples of successful hires who blossomed at our company:

Jon — from Recruiter to Senior Director of Sales

Résumé: Jon had just retired from the Air Force after 20 years of service. As commandant of an Air Force Leadership School, he'd basically been the leader of a school of leaders that taught future leaders.

Why We Hired Jon: Jon became available to us when he was moving his family back to his hometown of Erie, Pennsylvania to be closer to his aging parents. There's no doubt he was overqualified to be a recruiter. That job includes running employment ads, screening résumés, and conducting pre-employment tests and a brief first interview. Asking why candidate after candidate had left a previous job wasn't a challenge for this former police investigator. We hired Jon because we had an immediate need for a recruiter and believed he was the kind of leader who could play a key role in our long-term growth plans.

Jon Developed Into: The senior director of sales of our $10 million IT publishing division, helping to grow each team's sales by developing the people skills of the sales managers who reported to him. At first, salespeople were skeptical of their recruiter-turned-sales-boss, but Jon won them over with his low-key demeanor and servant leadership approach. Don't believe me? Here are a handful of sales employees' comments from one of Jon's recent annual reviews:
- "If I need someone to talk to, I feel like I can talk to Jon. I like when he's in our meetings and walks through our cubicles. I truly believe he cares about us and how we're doing personally as much as professionally."

- "He listens. And when he talks, it's about *what* is right, not *who* is right. He is also understanding and realizes not everyone is cut from the same cloth."
- "I never feel like he tries to use his title to get his way. He's very good at being unbiased — looking at the facts and helping you make a decision on what's right."
- "He treats everyone fairly and with humility. He's good at speaking with intense candor to get his point across but does it in a way that inspires you to fix the problem."
- "Jon provides me the ideal balance of someone that I really enjoy working for, someone I really respect, someone I learn a lot from, and someone that isn't afraid to point out the areas that people need to work on. Jon is always willing to give me time when I need it, especially when it is an issue he can tell is frustrating me."
- "Jon is an exceptional employee and man. Wow, that guy has a strong heart and works his butt off to do what is right and never complains. I always try to look around the office and recognize a trait or two that people have I would like to learn from. With Jon, there are numerous traits."

Boy, Am I Glad We: Hired a person with temperance (emotional control), kindness, and fortitude. Sales creates hurricanes of emotions, but Jon's outstanding character traits helped him achieve business outcomes while taking care of his people. He also saves me time as company president. With Jon on the job, our sales team requires less of my personal personnel intervention.

Ed — from Editor to Publishing Director

Résumé: Ed worked as sports information director at a small private local college and, to make ends meet, tended bar on the weekends. Lots of hours, little pay.

Why We Hired Ed: Ed joined the Jameson team prior to my coming on board, so I take zero credit for hiring him. The company owners hired Ed because of his writing experience and Puritan work ethic. His strong ties to our city and engaging personality were a plus.

Ed Developed Into: A model chief editor and key member of our company's Steering Committee. At first, Ed didn't know much about business or the technologies he was tasked to write about. But because of his insatiable intellectual curiosity and roll-up-your-sleeves work ethic, he soon became regarded as an authority in the IT world. Ed didn't just bang out copy for us; he changed the markets we worked in. Despite a heavy writing workload, he willingly shouldered the burden of launching a second magazine for our company. It was natural to promote him to chief editor of that new publication. And it was natural for Ed to not rest for a moment. Within a couple years of launching the new magazine, he helped lead the charge to spin off another profitable publication. To maximize Ed's abilities, we moved him into the position of publishing director. In plain language, he's the supervisor of all our chief editors, providing a seasoned sounding board for their ideas. In his role as a Steering Committee member, we like that Ed's not just a good thinker, but that his brain is connected to his mouth. He regularly challenges the owners of our company and other senior managers about our business practices and our plans for the future.

Boy, Am I Glad We: Had a mission to grow our company so we could make room for a capable person like Ed. I'm equally glad we found someone with Ed's rare combination of ambition and humility. Though Ed has been lauded for his accomplishments and invited to speak at numerous national conferences, he's remained down to earth. It's pretty cool to see someone of his stature bring to work a plastic food container filled with brisket for an employee who couldn't pack his own lunch that day.

Sarah — from Editorial Intern to Chief Editor

Résumé: Sarah had very little professional experience. She had been working hard as a restaurant server and bartender while attending school full time to earn her MBA at a nearby Penn State branch campus.

Why We Hired Sarah: Sarah was recommended to us by a co-worker who was an MBA classmate of hers. This co-worker knew Sarah didn't have writing or sales experience, but noticed that she possessed the valuable character traits of ambition, work ethic, perseverance, and responsibility. Unsure if Sarah would enjoy her first office job, we created an intern position in our editorial department as a way of giving her a tryout with our team.

Sarah Developed Into: The chief editor of one of our product groups, leading the team into fertile markets, winning over some big-name customers, and even changing the name of one of our magazines to reflect the needs of the market. Her path to success wasn't paved with gold from the outset, though. Soon after we hired Sarah as a full-time editor, the Great Recession of 2008 slammed our company and we furloughed several employees. We didn't want to lose Sarah. She'd mentioned during the interview process that she'd be open to trying sales, so we offered her that opportunity. Sarah learned that she didn't like direct sales much, but she didn't quit at the first sign of adversity. She persisted and moved back to an editor position when we broke into a new market.

Boy, Am I Glad We: Hired a person with ambition and perseverance. A lesser person wouldn't have withstood that level of adversity. Sarah took the long-term view and pressed on.

Tim — from Account Executive to Director of Sales

Résumé: Tim had just graduated with a marketing degree from Penn State and worked evenings cleaning offices.

Why We Hired Tim: Would you have hired Tim for a high-level sales job based on his résumé? Most people wouldn't. But we offered Tim a job because his life beyond work proved that he possessed responsibility and humility. Nobody I know really *wants* to clean offices — especially while going to school full time — but Tim did both because he was supporting his newborn child and fiancée. We also felt we owed Tim an interview because of how we met him. When our company representative arrived at the campus where Tim's college was hosting a job fair, she couldn't find a local newspaper to purchase. Students and faculty members walked past her. But Tim saw she was lost, offered directions, and walked with her to find a paper.

Tim Developed Into: One of our best-ever account executives. His unassuming, inquisitive, low-pressure approach to prospects was endearing and allowed him to gather facts that helped him make the sale. Lots of sales. Tim's interest in his customers was evident in his candid conversations with them. He didn't just try to *sell* them; he genuinely *helped* them. Tim also believes in helping his teammates, so he volunteered to take on responsibilities beyond his sales job. We eventually moved him into the role of sales manager, where he excelled again. He not only offered practical advice to his direct reports, he brought to our management meetings the salesperson's perspective that other managers lacked. And, being as candid with us as he was with his customers, Tim spoke his mind when he disagreed with an action we were planning to take. Tim not only helped us make better decisions, he helped us effectively communicate changes to the entire sales team. Tim was a key player in eliminating an *us vs. them* attitude from our company.

Boy, Am I Glad We: Got lost looking for a paper at the job fair! And I'm glad we looked beyond Tim's thin résumé to learn what's inside him. He proved to be responsible to his family, his customers, his co-workers, and his employer.

As these examples illustrate, it's not wise to base your conclusions solely on a candidate's résumé. Many companies discard the résumé of any candidate who does not have specific job-related experience. This is typically a mistake. Those companies miss out on candidates who, if taught the necessary skills, could be excellent employees.

Identify lack of related experience as an aversion. In the first interview, ask probing questions to determine if the candidate's personality and character are comparable to what you want for that position. Inexperienced hiring managers — and even some veterans — often eliminate candidates who lack experience in the jobs they are applying for. That might be fine if you're hiring a doctor or a mechanic. But for many jobs, it's not the right tactic.

CHAPTER 3

What to Look for During the Interview

Your pre-employment interviews should be structured to determine if the candidate is a good match for your company in four areas:

- Skills
- Personality
- Character
- Mapping

Candidates need to prove during the interview process that they meet your standard in *all* four areas or could quickly attain acceptable levels of performance. Each interviewer in your hiring process needs to learn what's in the person to know if that candidate will meet your target.

What does it mean to learn what's *in* the person (vs. what the person has done)? I like what John Taffer of Bar Rescue said in an Inc. Magazine interview. Taffer and his company frequently turn around struggling restaurants and bars, with people the core of the success. "Unless you focus on the human element, your company will struggle," Taffer said. "You give me someone with the right [qualities], and I'll give you a bar manager in three weeks. You give me someone who has been a lousy bar manager for 30 years, and in three weeks, you'll still have a lousy bar manager."

Examples of my own hiring mistakes will clarify this concept:

Skill Deficiency

Catherine, a candidate for a writer position for one of our IT magazines, was likeable, presented well, and provided multiple examples of hard work and high character behavior. Every staff member who met her believed she'd interact well with co-workers and customers. She did. However, Catherine had poor writing skills; during the year she was employed with us, her stories were polluted with unclear, run-on sentences. Our only exposure to her writing ability in the pre-employment process was a brief essay that we asked all candidates to write. She had been a television reporter in college and for her entire professional career before joining us, so she had never proven she could write an in-depth case study or produce a substantive 2,000-word feature story.

In spite of her struggles to write, Catherine was upbeat and hardworking. Customers who met her at trade shows adored her. We loved a lot of what she did. But after extensive training (even sitting for hours at a time with the retired chairman of a local college English department), she couldn't get the whole job done.

Had we required Catherine to prove during our interview process that she could meet our skill requirement, we would have realized that she'd have been unlikely to advance along our learning curve at an acceptable rate and acquire the necessary skills for our job. We wouldn't have offered her the job, which would have saved us significant time and money. And let's not forget about the employee, who wasted a year of her professional life moving down the wrong career path. Catherine's now successful in another line of work.

Personality Deficiency

To solve the issue detailed in the Skill Deficiency example, we implemented a day-long writing test for any editorial candidate. So that perfected our hiring process, right? I wish it were that easy. This story is about Scott, a candidate who aced the writing test. I mean he nailed it. Years have gone by since he took his writing test, and no one has come close to his performance. He was great on paper, but his interactions with co-workers around the office and with customers at trade shows were a different story. The guy was an introvert, and we were asking him to walk into a cocktail reception and introduce himself to strangers. If he'd wanted to freelance for us from home, we'd have loaded him up with assignments. But he quit a few months into the job in part because he was frustrated with us pushing him outside his comfort zone.

What mistake did I make as the hiring manager? During the interview process, I sensed Scott was an introvert. He didn't quiver when he shook my hand or flinch when I asked him a question, but he certainly didn't impress me as someone I'd enjoy going to lunch with a couple times a month. Instead of doing the right thing — giving him multiple chances to display his personality and letting the results speak for themselves — I asked co-workers who met Scott if they found his personality to be a problem. Nobody was offended by him, so we hired him.

The editor who trained Scott at his first trade show pulled me aside after they came back from the road and told me about the remedial interpersonal training he had to give our new hire. So not only did the new guy not perform well, we were sapping one of our strongest editors of his time and ability to interact with important customers. I sensed that Scott wasn't right for our job, but I let his writing skills blind me to his personality deficiency.

That was a mistake hire. When judging a candidate's personality, I now multiply any quirks by 2,080, the number of hours in 52 40-hour workweeks. Then I ask myself, "Can I stand that?" If the answer is *no*, we thank the candidate for meeting with us and terminate the pre-employment process.

Character Deficiency

Thomas Jefferson didn't tell me this directly, but legend has it he once said, "The *second* prerequisite for being hired is education and talent to do the job; the *first* is high character." Don't think of character as honesty alone. Honesty is an important character trait, but there's more to good character than being forthright. Here are the criteria we examine when assessing someone's complete character:

1. <u>Prudence</u>: Doesn't make reckless choices. Lacks prejudice. Keeps things in perspective.
2. <u>Justice</u>: Doesn't advantage self, family, or friends at the expense of others.
3. <u>Fortitude</u>: Demonstrates moral courage. Does the hard thing. Encounters adversity or bears pain with a pleasant disposition.
4. <u>Temperance</u>: Exhibits self-discipline, emotional control, and thrift. Confronts personal failings; doesn't excuse them.
5. <u>Ambition</u>: Is driven by desire to realize personal potential and improve self, your organization, and society.
6. <u>Work Ethic</u>: Channels action toward a defined purpose. Demonstrates initiative, determination to succeed, and quality workmanship.
7. <u>Perseverance</u>: Maintains focus and single-minded persistence in spite of obstacles. Exhibits endurance. Takes the long-term view.

8. Honesty: Practices full disclosure, candor, and fidelity. Is sincere and pure of heart. Pays debts on time.
9. Kindness: Considers feelings of others. Takes genuine interest in people. Is compassionate.
10. Responsibility: Is decisive and self-reliant; a dutiful grown child, sibling, spouse, parent, and employee.
11. Service: Is a good steward and peacemaker. Encourages others. Promotes harmony.
12. Ongoing Education: Engages in a lifelong process of introspection, searching, self-improvement, learning, and knowledge application.
13. Enthusiasm: Exudes optimism, cheerfulness, energy, and a belief in being able to influence outcomes.
14. Humility: Is willing to admit personal faults, apologize, accept criticism, and give credit where credit is due.
15. Respectfulness: Has self-respect and treats others with courtesy and dignity. Is punctual. Does not use foul language.
16. Gratitude: Shows appreciation. Counts blessings.
17. Loyalty: Is dedicated to noble people and high ideals. Has enduring relationships.
18. Generosity: Charitably interprets the actions of others. Gives with no expectation of return.

Before I detail a failed hire in terms of character deficiency, let me brag about Nyki. One of our best hires ever, Nyki was brought on as a production manager, replaced me as managing editor, and then replaced me again as operations manager. Nyki had a rare ability to be flexible when appropriate and hold the line when necessary. Her co-workers adored her no matter what course of action she chose.

When Nyki's husband, a physician, was invited to become a partner in an out-of-town practice, she gave her quit notice nearly two years before her departure. That allowed her to actively participate in hiring Timothy to take her spot. He had tons of experience managing a large staff of operations employees and shared with us multiple examples of using sound judgment. He was bright-eyed and upbeat in the interview process. One of his interviews took place on the same day as our monthly company lunch. (All Jameson employees break bread together, and we hand out awards to top performers.) If we had pom-poms, Timothy would have grabbed them and shouted, "Whoo-hoo!" after attending the lunch.

The biggest deficiency our interview process uncovered was his ego. Timothy made several statements that crossed the line between confidence and egotism. When we talked with him about a potential ego problem, he accepted the criticism and promised to do better. Together, we came up with an action plan that we felt would keep his ego in check. But he lasted only six weeks before we asked him to leave our company.

While I identified that ego was a problem, I didn't get to the manifestation of the problem. You might be thinking that Timothy lacked humility. But when we pointed out that his inflated ego was an issue, he was quick to talk with us about solving the problem. The real problem was Timothy's *kindness deficiency*. For example, we asked him to go to lunch with his new co-workers to get to know them better. They each reported that he talked about himself ad nauseam; he lacked genuine interest in them. After almost every meeting we had, instead of asking if we achieved the outcome, he asked, "How'd I do?"

Here's how bad it got: Five weeks into the job, Timothy joined seven co-workers on a car trip to visit our out-of-state printer. At a rest stop on the way back, people in Timothy's car were offering those in the other car up to $50 to switch vehicles. Timothy and our company parted ways just days later.

Mapping Deficiency

Karla had just quit teaching — the only profession she'd ever known — and we felt lucky to hire her as a writer for one of our IT magazines. She appeared to be on the road to stardom after just a few months on the job. She grasped the technical aspect of business writing, and her stories really popped off the page. Her vibrant personality was evident in her writing, her phone conversations with customers, and her meetings with co-workers and supervisors.

One problem: Karla didn't like our job. I remember her coming to me to talk about her struggles. It was a pleasant conversation but she told me matter-of-factly, "I really like the company. The people are great. I just don't like business or writing. And I don't want to be in sales. Is there maybe another position in the company for me?" We talked through every position in the company, but none of them appealed to her. So we invited her to stay until we found her replacement or she found work elsewhere. Karla eventually found success as an educational administrator.

One more thing worth mentioning about Karla: On her final day as our employee, when you'd think she'd be mostly disengaged from our company and leave early, she worked overtime to finish a story. You hate to lose a good person like that. But I'd rather lose a good person than make them miserable working a job they're not mapped for.

Taking a minute right now to perform this exercise should make these deficiency concepts clearer:

1. List your failed hires.
2. Categorize each one's deficiency: skill, personality, character, or mapping. (Some have more than one.)
3. Write the appropriate category or categories next to each former employee's name.

It's OK to write in the margins of this book. Plus, if you end up being famous one day, your scribblings will make your copy super-valuable.

Balance skill, personality, character, and mapping

Interviewers often become mesmerized by experience, personality, or another single aspect and fail to recognize flaws that should disqualify a candidate. Examples of how one trait can blind an interviewer:

- *Skill:* "We're in the insurance business, and he sold insurance for seven years. We should hire him."
- *Personality:* "That guy was really funny. Customers would love hanging out with him."
- *Character:* "He's a volunteer in his church and spoke about how important family is to him. He's a solid citizen, so he would be good hire."
- *Mapping:* "He has tons of drive and wants to be challenged. He's built for management."

I made this mistake when our company was hiring a senior sales manager to mentor our sales management team and sales reps. Terrance had the kind of résumé we didn't see very often — more than two decades of sales management and sales experience, most of it for one of the world's leading telecommunications companies. He told us he'd achieved record sales and been promoted several times before deciding to leave the company. He'd traveled a lot and liked that our inside sales job would keep him closer to home. Terrance mentioned an ongoing dispute with his former employer, but we didn't dig for details. Why should we? The guy was a superstar! He looked the part, too, with his crisp suit and million-dollar smile. He also had an endearing English accent, plus natural charm. What could possibly go wrong? Almost everything.

Here are some of the lowlights I still can't erase from my brain:

- In his first week on the job, we had a group training session with the entire sales team. When someone asked for techniques to get an executive on the phone, Terrance said, "Make up a name and title. Tell them you're someone else." The room was silent. His advice was the opposite of honesty, a character trait our company values.
- We asked Terrance to familiarize himself with our sales reps and help them sell by tagging their calls several hours a day. (He'd listen to the conversation live, but the rep and customer couldn't hear him.) When I asked in our weekly meeting how that was going, he said, "Fine." When I pressed for details, he didn't have any. "They don't make any calls for me to listen to," he eventually confessed. "I just sit there." When I asked what he said to the reps he claimed weren't making calls, he protested that wasn't his job. Lots of character failures on this one — fortitude, honesty, responsibility, and work ethic.
- As you can imagine, Terrance struggled in his new job. He said it so beat him up emotionally that he wanted to take a day off to get his mind straight. "No problem," we said. One day turned into two, but he swore he'd be back the next day. Two turned into three, but he was going to be here Friday for sure. Guess what happened on Friday? Terrance called to say that a friend invited him to an out-of-state Saturday-afternoon college football game and they'd be driving all day. Take your pick of character failures here — prudence, temperance, ambition, work ethic, perseverance, kindness, responsibility, service, respectfulness, loyalty.
- Terrance came back to work the next week and vowed he'd try his darnedest. He and I met together privately, and we wrote a detailed list with clear expectations. He couldn't miss any more work except for illness. He'd have to tag calls and give reps proper direction. He was 100% in agreement that he could do the job and would enjoy it. Terrance had a good day or two, then left me an early morning voice mail saying he couldn't be in because his wife was very sick. I called repeatedly to see what was the matter, but he didn't pick up. That afternoon, I heard an intercom page: "Terrance, your wife is on hold for you." We told her we'd thought he was with her. She said he should be at work. Hmmmm. In our next conversation, Terrance gave his immediate quit notice.

My mistake was getting caught up in Terrance's outstanding skills and personality and paying zero attention to his character. I'll say this many times in this book: **Your interview questions need to drill down on skill, personality, character, <u>and</u> mapping.** Three out of four isn't good enough. You've got to know if the candidate is the right fit for the position and your company in *every* respect.

I've detailed many of my hiring failings. So you might be thinking, "Why'd I buy a book written by such a loser?" We all make hiring mistakes — you, me, your favorite boss — everybody. I recall hearing a podcast by Jack Welch, the ultrasmart and ultrasuccessful former GE chairman and CEO, who said he got hiring right 50% of the time. In *Jack: Straight From The Gut*, Welch laments some of his hiring mistakes: "The inconsistency of my first hires was laughable. One of my most common errors was to hire on appearances. In marketing, I'd sometimes recruit good-looking, slick-talking packages. Some of those were good, but some were just empty suits. … In the early days I fell in love with great résumés filled with degrees in different disciplines. They could be bright and intellectually curious, but they often turned out to be unfocused dabblers, unwilling to commit, lacking intensity and passion for any one thing. In the hands of the inexperienced, résumés are dangerous weapons."

Even a business genius like Welch struggled to do better than a coin flip. Finding and hiring the right person for your organization is difficult. You will increase your chances of success if your interview process drills down on skills, personality, character, <u>and</u> mapping.

Don't eliminate a candidate for not being an "angel." Many of my company's best employees have committed egregious mistakes with past employers. Some were fired. Probe to determine if candidates have learned from those mistakes and changed their behavior accordingly.

You should also probe to determine if the candidate's actions and attitudes could be reactions to the atmosphere of a previous workplace. Take Pat, for example. We identified as an aversion his criticism of his previous employer, who had let Pat go a few months prior. Pat didn't communicate the company's flaws inappropriately to us. But he alluded to so *many* flaws — plus he'd been terminated — that we thought much of the problem could be him.

When I performed the reference check, Pat's former supervisor used phrases like *negative person, frequent complainer,* and *bad attitude.* But when I pressed for details, she revealed that Pat pointed out fundamental business flaws that management didn't like hearing. Long story short, this screwed-up company went out of business a couple years after my chat with that manager. And Pat had a successful near-decade run with our company.

CHAPTER 4

Behavior-Focused Interviewing

*B*ehavior-focused interviewing centers on the belief that past behavior is the best predictor of future conduct. During your interviews, seek to uncover a pattern of recurring behaviors. In general, here's how:

- **Ask open-ended, past-tense questions** like: *What exactly did you say to him?*
- **Don't use theoretical questions** like: *How do you typically handle tough customers?* Instead, ask a behavior-focused question like: *Can you give me an example of how you handled a tough customer?*
- **Don't ask leading questions** like: *Did you do that to motivate the group?* Ask the behavior-focused version: *Why did you do that?*
- **Don't provide leading information** like: *We look for candidates who are committed to working here for 10 years or more.* Candidates will ask you questions about the job. Be cordial, but don't tip your hand by giving information that will coach them on how to answer your questions.
- **Don't ask close-ended questions** like: *Would you say you're comfortable having hard conversations?* Use the behavior-focused approach: *How do you feel after having a hard conversation?*

Depending on the situation and outcome you are striving to achieve, some theoretical, leading, and close-ended interview questions can be appropriate. But you need to recognize their limitations. If you eliminate behavior-focused questions in favor of theoretical, leading, and close-ended questions, you will never learn what's in the person. And you will make bad hiring decisions.

It is a mistake to hire candidates based only on their promises. Don't believe them when they say, "I'm a'gonna ..." Skeptically validate their answers with behavior-focused questions.

The tone of your interview should be more of a conversation, not an interrogation. If the hiring manager's questions are too serious and too direct, candidates will keep their guard up. To break down the wall between you and the candidate, your tone and demeanor should be non-threatening.

- Get a full understanding of the situation by asking open-ended questions like: *Can you explain what's going on with ...?* or *Can you help me understand ...?*

- Listen carefully to the answers. If you think you missed something, ask the same question in another way.

- Read body language and mannerisms to get a feel for how much you can trust what candidates are saying. Do they seem calm or nervous? Do they look at you when speaking or avoid eye contact? Are they fidgety or still? Do they seem confident in what they are saying?

Do not base your final opinion of the candidate on just one or two data points. One instance of a specific attitude or behavior does not constitute a trend, and filling in the blanks with your assumptions is a mistake. Ask probing questions to fully understand the situation and any reasons for the candidate's behavior.

Example: During the past five years, the candidate has worked two different jobs. She says if we hire her, she is unsure she will still be with our company 10 years from now.

Incorrect technique: The interviewer assumes the candidate is a job hopper and will not stay with the company for at least 10 years.

Correct technique: The interviewer asks, "Why are you unsure you'll be here in 10 years?" The candidate responds that one company she'd worked at recently was sold and another moved out of town. She also mentions that her father has worked in pharmaceutical sales for 25 years, dealing with frequent and numerous mergers and company buyouts. The candidate has been researching to find a good company to which she can devote her career and from which she will eventually retire — like her grandfather did — but those companies are hard to find in today's business climate. The candidate also mentions that she is so earnest about working for a stable company that she turned down a start-up's lucrative job offer.

Keep your emotions under control — or you won't find what you're looking for. Discernment requires self-control. If your emotions get the best of you during an interview, you will make bad decisions. You should be happy to have the candidate join your team; at the same time, you should also be searching for a reason to eliminate each candidate as quickly as you can. Stick to facts and truths, not feelings.

Understand that you — yes, you — control the interview. Candidates should be nervous or emotional because two people will leave the conference room at the end of the interview, and only one of them runs the risk of not having a job with your company.

Ways that emotions could negatively affect your decision making:

- The candidate and hiring manager are about the same age and share similar interests. The manager hires the candidate because "I like him. We got along great."

- The hiring manager is stressed due to understaffing, so the manager lowers the hiring standard to fill the seat.

- On a very busy day, the hiring manager shortens the interview by asking only superficial questions and does not invest the necessary time to ask probing follow-up questions.

- The hiring manager views interviewing as a necessary evil, not a core element of his job, and does not adequately prepare for the interview.

One emotion-induced mistake hiring managers often make is hiring someone who is likeable instead of someone who also has the skills, character, and mapping to do the job. These misguided hiring decisions generally result in a short and frustrating career for the candidate. On the company side, heavy management labor is wasted on futile attempts to get the employee up to speed.

I almost made that mistake when my company was looking for a chief editor, one of the more important positions in a publishing company. One candidate was bright, freelanced for Inc. Magazine, had a strong business-writing background, and had local roots. His candid answers showed charisma and professionalism. I liked all those attributes, plus we needed a chief editor ASAP. I found myself rooting for him to give good answers to our questions, but I didn't allow my emotions to get in the way of our decision making. The candidate was unsure of where he wanted to steer his career path and, after several interviews, he and our hiring team concluded that our chief editor position wasn't the job for him.

Everything worked out for the best. That candidate took a job in the banking industry, and we hired an editor who grew into a wonderful chief editor. We're thrilled with the guy we hired. He's taken the job to new levels, and he plans to spend the rest of his career with us.

Two simple proven ways to maintain self-control:

1. Think after the candidate speaks. Use silence to your advantage. Decide how you want to handle the situation, then act.

2. Take thorough notes. There will be times when you initially feel enthusiastic about someone you've interviewed. Then you'll go through your notes and realize that the candidate's answers lacked substance. Answer after answer reveals nothing special in the candidate, an aversion temporarily masked by their enjoyable personality.

In general, probing for specific aversions and basing your decisions on a balance of skill, personality, character, and mapping will help you avoid losing emotional control.

Conduct pre-employment tests

Pre-employment tests assess a candidate's cognitive abilities and personality traits. The results should be measured against testing guidelines and successful employees' tests. Your goal is to hire candidates whose cognitive ability and personality traits are similar to those of successful employees. While not 100% predictive, pre-employment tests can be a strong indicator of a candidate's strengths and potential aversions. They can guide you toward what to ask that candidate in an interview.

The Wonderlic Cognitive Ability Test and DISC behavioral test have served my company well. I won't go into a ton of detail here on Wonderlic or DISC, because there's plenty of information about them online. Determine which tests work best for *your* business. "We don't need tests" isn't an acceptable attitude. They are valuable tools in your hiring arsenal.

I guarantee some candidates will protest the tests. I think their griping is great! It ties in with behavior-focused interviewing. The appropriate candidate response to pre-employment tests is something like "No problem. I'll roll up my sleeves and get it done." That's how you want an in-earnest employee to behave. Conversely, if the candidate is incredulous about taking the tests, you've gained insight into how that person might react if asked to follow an unfamiliar process as an employee. Pre-test excuses about not testing well afford you more insight into how candidates react when pushed outside their comfort zone.

We've even had candidates comment that taking our tests was "a stupid waste of time." We didn't ask them to join our team. That would have been a stupid waste of time.

Conduct multiple interviews

At its core, the pre-employment process involves getting important information on the table, sorting through it, and making a decision. Some hiring managers think they need to gather a bucketful of information before hiring a candidate. Others think it's more like two buckets. They're all selling themselves short. In actuality, you need a wheelbarrow overflowing with data to draw a clear picture of any candidate. The more information you can uncover and the more skillfully you analyze it, the better your hiring decision will be.

Multiple interviews give the hiring manager the opportunity to reflect on the candidate's answers and prepare targeted follow-up questions for the next interview. They also give the candidate (and the candidate's family) a chance to reflect on leaving a current employer, changing careers, working for your company, etc.

Multiple interviews allow the hiring manager to observe whether the candidate's answers and behaviors remain consistent and to compare and contrast various candidates.

Multiple interviews help you assess fortitude and perseverance. Can candidates endure answering multiple questions and having their answers validated? Or are they easily frustrated? This process tests candidates' desire for the job and desire to work for your company. A candidate who isn't sufficiently committed will take another job without first asking if your hiring process can be expedited. Quite frankly, it's better to lose that candidate at that stage than three months into the job when a "better employer" comes calling.

My company has learned that because most companies don't conduct multiple interviews, candidates tend to think we're nuts when we ask them to sit down with us maybe five or six times. Unfamiliar with the best practice of multiple interviews, most candidates are accustomed to a handshake, a résumé review, a nice chat, then (hopefully) a job offer. You will need to explain how multiple interviews benefit candidates as well as your company. They will get to know your company as well as you get to know them. That's important when making a life-changing decision like choosing a new employer.

I make these comments to help candidates understand why we interview them over and over (and over):

- "During the week, you often spend more time at work than with your spouse. How much time did you spend with your spouse before you popped the question? How many times did you go out before you decided this was 'the one'? If you proposed after one or two dates, your family would have thought you were moving too fast. Your relationship with your employer isn't as important, but work is a major influence on your life, and we don't want either one of us to be impulsive with this decision."

- "Let's say we conduct six 2 1/2-hour interviews with you. That's a total of 15 hours. If you come on board, by the end of the day Tuesday of your first week, you'll have spent more time working at our company than being interviewed by us. I'm guessing that come Wednesday morning, you won't feel like you're an expert on our job. After your first year with us, you'll have worked about 2,000 hours. So investing 15 hours — or 0.0075% of your first year — before we make the job offer seems prudent."

When in doubt, schedule another interview. "When in doubt, throw 'em out" used to be my motto. Pretty catchy, isn't it? But it was incorrect thinking. Eliminating a candidate without fully understanding the situation and skeptically validating all the facts could cause you to lose an excellent potential employee. To translate that into specific dollars for my company, consider that one account executive could develop a new sales territory yielding more than $1 million in revenue.

If you are on the fence after your initial meeting, bring the candidate back for the next step in the interview process. The only loss you'll suffer is maybe two hours out of your day. Here's my new motto: "A candidate who is not a definite 'no,' is a 'yes' to bring back for another interview." If the candidate could *possibly* perform up to standard within a reasonable time frame, schedule the candidate for another interview.

My new motto is more cumbersome, for sure (it won't fit on a T-shirt), but it's wiser advice.

CHAPTER 5

Emotional Outcomes

As I stated previously, the intended business outcome of your interviews should be to determine if the candidate is a good match for your company in terms of skills, personality, character, and mapping. But achieving desired business outcomes is only part of the equation. Emotional outcomes are also important. Consider this extreme (but true) story:

Jayson was a candidate for an open editor position at our company. Because he lived about two hours from our office, we scheduled the interview for 10 a.m. so he wouldn't have to leave home at the crack of dawn. When Jayson wasn't at our office at 10 on the dot, I asked our receptionist to call my extension the minute he walked in. Nearly 20 minutes passed before my phone rang. "I just gave him the application," the receptionist said. "He got here at 10:17." She called back a couple minutes later to let me know that Jayson had completed his application and was ready for our interview.

I greeted him, and we walked to the conference room together. He didn't apologize for being late or anything like that. I even asked how traffic was, and he said there'd been no problems. I was dying to address him being late, but didn't want to challenge the guy 39 seconds after meeting him. So I asked standard questions about his job search, his goals for the next two or three years, and the most difficult thing about his current job. Then we talked about some of the difficult parts of our job. Our standard work hours are a stumbling block for some candidates. We don't work on flextime; all operations employees are required to be working by 8 o'clock. He said that wouldn't be a problem, and that gave me an opening.

"What time was this interview scheduled to begin?" I asked. It was a sincere question. Our recruiter might have mistakenly told him the interview was to start at 10:30. But his reply was "10 o'clock." So I asked, "What time did you get here? What time did you walk in the door?"

"Just a couple minutes after. Maybe 10:05," he replied.

"I think it was later than that."

"No ... it was ... just after 10," he said sheepishly.

"I asked our receptionist to call me right after you walked in, and she said that was at 10:17."

"OK."

"Here's why I bring that up, Jayson. Our attendance policy requires you to be working by 8 o'clock each morning. Not just in the building by 8, but *working* by 8. If you walk in the door at 8, you're late. I just want to make sure you can follow that policy and not be late regularly. You might think that's a little anal, but that's how ..."

"I don't <u>think</u> you're anal — you <u>are</u> anal!" he shouted.

He was as angry as I've ever seen a candidate. He ranted about how unfair and inconsiderate employers are. He even criticized his ex-girlfriend's refusal to testify on his behalf when he sued his former employer (who was, like my company, a publisher).

So here's my situation in a nutshell: A litigious, seething candidate I had no intention of hiring was sitting across from me. If I ended the interview on that note, he'd leave angry because he'd driven two hours only to be harangued by a nitwit manager. He'd already sued one employer. So why wouldn't he call the EEOC to file a discrimination claim against my company? And even if he didn't go the legal route, he'd certainly complain about us to anyone who cared to listen.

For the next hour, I focused 100% on achieving the emotional outcome of Jayson leaving our office calm and with no ill will against us. My questions shifted to subjects he'd enjoy talking about. As a reporter, what's the most interesting story he ever wrote? What efforts did he put in to make that story special? What's a goal he was proud of achieving? What tasks did he like performing the most? To make our interaction conversational, I used comments, facial expressions, and body language that encouraged him to keep telling his stories. He was a pretty colorful character once he settled down.

And I didn't even have to end the interview. He said something to the effect of, "Well, I know you're not going to hire me. But I hope you had a good time talking with me today." I told him I enjoyed our conversation. "Me, too," he replied.

I hope that extreme example of an emotional interview outcome drives home the point that no matter how strong certain candidates are or how obvious their lack of qualifications, you want every candidate to feel certain emotional outcomes.

Here are six emotional outcomes your interview process should strive to achieve:

1. **The candidate feels your company is professional.** You will be judged on many criteria:
   - The appearance of the interviewers and your facility.
   - The interviewer's handshake and eye contact.
   - Your timely correspondence. How soon after receiving a candidate's résumé do you respond? Do you return emails and phone calls in a timely fashion? Do you follow up within 48 hours of an interview? Or do you leave candidates hanging and not follow up at all?
   - The time you allocate for an interview. Do eliminated candidates perceive they are being rushed out of your office?
   - Your posture, eye contact, facial expressions, and attentiveness during the interview.
   - Your word being good. If you say you'll call a candidate within a week, do you actually call? If you say you'll meet with a candidate at 1 p.m., are you ready at that time?
   - The length of your interview process. Is there unnecessary lag time between interviews? Is your process unnecessarily redundant? Do interviewers ask the same basic questions about things like salary history, job-related responsibilities, and personal strengths? How do you feel when you fill out a 100-question health history in your doctor's office, then do it all over again at a testing facility the next day?
   - Your treatment of candidates eliminated from your process. Do you call them or expect them to call you? Do you deliver the message clearly? What is the tone of the "knockout" phone call? Eliminated candidates should feel like the job was not a good fit for them, not like failures or as if you're giving them the runaround.

2. **The candidate's questions were answered**. Take time during each interview to ask if the candidate has any questions. Answer in detail, but without giving information that will suggest how to answer subsequent questions.

   If your process involves multiple interviewers, make sure they communicate with each other and share consistent data. You don't want one interviewer saying the training program typically takes six weeks and another saying the duration is closer to six months. If the candidate has a question you can't answer on the spot (such as details about your short-term disability benefit), bring in the employee who has that information. Or let the candidate know how soon you can provide it. (Then deliver that information before the date you promised!)

3. **The candidate was happy to interview with you**. Remember that the tone of your interview should be more of a conversation than an interrogation. The interviewer should be warm and friendly. Ask warm-up questions before beginning your actual interview. Even if you've determined you will eliminate the candidate, conclude with innocuous, cool-down questions. Examples: *I've asked a lot of questions. Do you have any for me? Are you heading back to work now or do you have the rest of the day off?*

   Despite your best efforts, not everyone will go away happy. Objectively reflect upon what you did. If you're satisfied that you acted appropriately, you've done your job ... no matter how loud eliminated candidates may scream.

4. **The candidate was exposed to the difficulties of the job**. See how the candidate reacts. Are they scared off by the reality of the job? Or eager to embrace the biggest challenge of their career? The all-time best answer I've received came just after I exposed a candidate to the difficulties of the job, then asked, "Are you ready for the biggest challenge of your career?" The typical answer is a fairly unemotional "yes." This candidate said, "I'm primed for it!" He's gone on to have a long and prosperous career at our company, and he successfully endured many struggles along the way.

5. **The candidate is sold on your job and your company.** Be realistic about the struggles the candidate will face on the job, but emphasize that the rewards for hard work are great. The more aggressive your questions and statements become, the more empathetic you must be. Or, said more plainly, the carrot should be bigger than the stick.

When you push candidates away, you have to provide info that will pull them in a bit more strongly:

> Incorrect way to push a candidate away: Drop the name of the ultimate hiring decision maker (such as your boss or the company owner) to test whether a sales candidate will call that person. Eliminate, without investigation, any candidate who doesn't call the hiring decision maker within a week. Guess whether the candidate's lack of initiative is due to low drive, lack of hardiness, fear of going upline, or something else.

> Correct example: Drop the name of the ultimate hiring decision maker to test whether a sales candidate will call that person. Schedule another interview with a candidate who doesn't call the hiring decision maker within a week. Ask benign questions to get a full understanding of why the candidate didn't pick up on your cue to go upline. Discuss how that lack of initiative will negatively impact the candidate's career and that improving to standard in that area could be the start of a successful sales career. You can even give another test to see if the candidate will go upline.

Overuse of pushing candidates away is a problem my company encountered during the years when we did a poor job of training hiring managers. Eliminated candidates should feel that they missed a good opportunity that just wasn't a fit for them. There should be no confusion or hard feelings. Candidates to whom you extend a job offer should be excited to come aboard.

6. **Their expectations were managed properly.** Candidates you want to advance in your interview process should feel that you are excited to have them as potential hires. Candidates you want to eliminate from your process should not mistakenly feel that they've been guaranteed another interview or a job. They should be aware of your biggest aversion(s) —unless sharing that information would unnecessarily create hard feelings.

Let me give a couple examples to clarify that last statement. (We'll talk more later about aversions and exposing aversions.)

Examples of safe-to-share aversions:
- The job requires previous supervision of employees, and the candidate has no supervisory experience or has expressed little desire to supervise.
- The candidate plans to move out of town in six months, and your job isn't mobile.

Example of aversions you *wouldn't* share:
- The candidate had poor professional presentation such as bad breath, greasy hair, or a limp handshake.
- A co-worker informs you just before the interview that when they worked together, the candidate was rude to co-workers and belligerent to supervisors.

If you dig deep enough, you should be able to uncover safe-to-share aversions for any candidate.

CHAPTER 6

Hiring Rules of Thumb

A *rule of thumb* is a principle whose broad application is not intended to be strictly accurate or reliable in every situation. It is an easily learned and easily applied procedure for *approximating* a determination. The following hiring principles grew out of mistakes my company made regarding whom and how we hired in the past and failure analyses performed to prevent future harm. If hiring managers at your company do a good job of failure analysis, they will be able to add new rules of thumb that further improve your outcomes. Likewise, some of these rules may become obsolete. Review these *Hiring Rules of Thumb,* then develop your own.

<u>Important:</u> When you ask questions to get a full understanding of the situation and the candidate's circumstances, the rule of thumb may not apply. But don't disregard a rule because it makes your job more difficult or because you don't understand its value. Establish a clear understanding throughout your organization — get inside the brains of everyone involved in the hiring process — about the *what* and the *why* behind your Hiring Rules of Thumb.

1. **Don't hire someone with below-average presentation.** If you are hiring for a position that requires interaction with customers, suppliers, or the public, hire someone with appropriate presentation. The successful candidate doesn't need to be a supermodel, but *must* exude professionalism. This goes beyond attire to include grooming, posture, grammar, a sparkle in the eye, enthusiasm, and a sense of substance. Customers want to buy from people like themselves. Hiring a 20-something kid

41

with facial piercings and tattoos to sell to corporate executives is a mistake. Your hire needs to fit in with your constituents.

2. **Offer jobs only to candidates you believe will still work at your company in 10 years.** There are no guarantees that an employee will stay with your company. But if you uncover reasons likely to cause a candidate to leave sooner, don't hire that person. You shouldn't be trying to put bodies in seats. You should be trying to hire the people who will create your future.

Any candidate may intend to work well past traditional retirement age, so don't automatically discount older candidates. Learn about their longevity goals, just like you would with any other candidate. Besides, age discrimination is illegal. You're not a crook, are you?

I recall one candidate who possessed many of the skills we were looking for. But when asked where she wanted to be in two or three years, she replied, "Anywhere but this town. I want to be in a big city." When we pressed for details, she said, "I just don't want to live in a town this size any more. I want to get a job in my field that will help me get something in Chicago or New York." We appreciated her honesty, but we didn't hire her.

On the flip side, two of our must successful employees — John and Jon — have worked in our company for nearly 20 years. Both are lifelong residents of Erie. And their spouses are from western Pennsylvania, reducing the chances they'd move out of town. They are both career salespeople (I think they'd break out in hives if they weren't influencing someone), and they've both advanced their careers in our sales organization.

An example of a rare exception to this rule of thumb would be hiring an entrepreneur-type who will work for you less than 10 years but, during that time, will make significant new sales and enter your company into new thriving markets.

3. **Don't hire candidates who frequently switch companies or careers.** A candidate whose résumé shows a pattern of jobs with less than four years' tenure will probably leave your company long before 10 years have passed. Some employees hop from job to job every two to four years. Other employees have a high job turnover because their employers are conducting some form of differentiation in which they terminate some

percentage of their bottom performers. Either cause is equally prob-
lematic for your goal of long employee tenure. But don't count switching companies against a candidate who lost a job because an employer
went bankrupt or closed down the candidate's location.

4. **Don't hire candidates who, while working at your company, would
    own, operate, manage, or assist with a sideline business.** If you can
    anticipate that a candidate's commitment to another business could be
    greater than their commitment to your company, there is a good prob-
    ability that your company will be harmed. Financial commitment to a
    sideline business could cause a candidate to act in the best interests of
    that business, not *your* business.

    Example: When we interviewed Yancey, we learned he was the owner
    of a small restaurant. When we expressed our concern, he assured us it
    wouldn't be a problem. He said he was technically the owner but his
    dad, who had bad credit and couldn't be the owner on paper, actually
    ran the place. We believed him — until Yancey started working for us.
    Yancey frequently came back from lunch late because he got caught up
    at the restaurant. Instead of making sales calls all morning, he spent
    time placing orders for the restaurant. And when you're placing orders
    instead of calling prospects, you don't make sales. Yancey's tenure with
    us was measured in months.

5. **Offer jobs only to a candidate whose family or whose spouse's fam-
    ily lives in or near the city where your office is located.** Odds are
    you'll lose employees who move back to their hometown upon the
    birth of their children or due to homesickness or parents' or in-laws'
    infirmity. This rule is not meant to discriminate on the basis of marital
    status. If an unmarried candidate is engaged to or living with a signifi-
    cant other, the likelihood of longevity with your company goes up if
    the candidate's or partner's parents live in your town. Chances of unat-
    tached candidates staying with your company increase if their parents
    live nearby.

    You might be furrowing your brow over this rule of thumb, wondering
    if it's wise or even legal to consider family in a hiring decision. This
    principle is meant to be intellectually inflammatory and challenge the
    hiring manager to fully understand a candidate. A candidate's family

situation is perhaps the most important factor in longevity at your company.

This principle has some history behind it:

- A manufacturing company in a rural area 25 miles from my hometown lost at least 10 executives as a result of ignoring this rule of thumb for several years. It was difficult to find executive-level candidates locally, so this company recruited candidates from all over the country. The candidates loved the new company and the bump to their pay, and their spouses promised to love the new town (even if the nearest shopping mall was 35 minutes away and the town's annual snowfall averaged 88 inches). But less than two years after accepting the job, every executive resigned because of a family situation — an ill parent, a homesick spouse, grandparents missing the kids, etc. This company should have invested time and money training junior executives with local roots.

- Before I joined Jameson Publishing, our owners hired a guy they envisioned becoming company president someday. He and his wife were from out of town, which was a major focus during the interview process. The candidate swore up and down that he'd never, ever, in a million years quit to move back home. He came on board and did an outstanding job. But guess what happened after the birth of his first child? He resigned to move nearer to family. So even if the non-local candidate sincerely expects to stay with your company for a long time, this rule of thumb predicts that the odds are against it.

- When my company was planning to grow by opening an office in Pittsburgh, two hours south of our Erie headquarters, a dozen employees initially said, "I'll move!" When we opened the office a year later, guess how many actually moved? Just four. The other eight wanted to stay close to extended family. And guess what each of the four who moved had in common? A spouse or significant other who grew up in the Pittsburgh area.

Don't overextend this rule of thumb to automatically eliminate a candidate who is not from your area. We hired Carin as an operations manager even though she grew up seven hours away, in Philadelphia, and her parents still lived there. We learned in our interview process that her husband was the second-generation owner of a local manufacturing company. If Carin wanted to move back home, her husband would have to sell the company and work for somebody else. Carin did a wonderful job for us. She left our company after about a half-decade of service, but she still lives in the area.

6. **Don't offer jobs to candidates who will have more than a 45-minute commute to your facility.** After the honeymoon period wears off, there's a high probability they'll start nagging you to let them work from home. And they'll insist that it's unreasonable to expect them to get to work on time. On bad-weather days, their 45-minute commute can turn into an hour or more … and who wants to endure *that* long term? There's a high likelihood that an employee whose commute takes more than 45 minutes will quit your company, citing the grief associated with that commute, and find a similar job closer to home.

7. **Don't offer a full-time job to a candidate whose history shows no financial need to work.** This also applies to a candidate who doesn't have to work full time or doesn't need a full-time salary to make ends meet. The probability is that these candidates will quit when the job becomes hard or frustrating.

8. **Maintain an anti-nepotism policy. Don't hire relatives of existing employees.** This rule of thumb is especially critical in relation to hiring relatives of managers and supervisors. If you don't follow it, the probability is that you will suffer employee dissension, incur unnecessary legal problems, and leave yourself open to accusations of cronyism (preferential treatment of relatives).

   This rule of thumb has worked for my company, but might not be applicable for small, family-owned businesses. I know of and have worked with many successful family businesses that break this rule. They all had clear guidelines for separation of work and family.

   Our owners wouldn't allow any of their five children to work in their existing businesses. That provided great solace for me and other company managers because we didn't have to look over our shoulders and wonder when "Junior" was going to show up and replace us.

   One of our employees wasn't as fortunate with his previous employer. Josh worked in HR, and the five brothers who owned the company frequently squabbled at work. I'm not sure if punches were ever thrown, but they swore and yelled at each other before storming out of meetings. One brother would give Josh direction, then another brother would stop by Josh's desk and say, "Forget him. Do this instead." How would you like to deal with that every day? If you introduce this atmosphere at your company, you'll lose good employees. But not your slacker nephew.

9. **Hold out for a candidate who fits your predetermined target.** Companies often run a predetermined number of recruitment advertisements and hire the "least-worst" candidate, even if all candidates fell short of the target. This rule of thumb implores you to continue recruiting for as long as it takes to find the candidate who meets or surpasses your standard.

One of my biggest hiring mistakes falls into this category. Despite the objections of two other hiring managers in our interview process, I thought we should give David a shot with our company. I could rationalize why David wasn't a terrible candidate for our open sales manager position, but he didn't meet our standard that our managers should be among "the ablest, most earnest, and reliable in the field of business." If I had followed that principle, I wouldn't have had data to justify hiring David. Shortly after we hired him, David failed as a sales manager. He later failed as an account executive. A couple months after he was terminated for lying to his manager about his daily sales contacts, I saw David at a local festival. He spotted me from about 20 yards away and quickly walked in the other direction.

10. **Hire the first candidate who matches your target, even if that is the first candidate through the process**. It's common for companies not to offer a job to a candidate until everyone in the process has been interviewed. This could cause you to miss out on an excellent candidate who got tired of waiting for you and took another job.

We'd just started looking for a recruiter when Jon applied for the job. After interviewing him, our operations manager tracked me down and said, "This guy has the kind of character we want in our company. I don't know what else is on your schedule tomorrow, but you're interviewing him." The urgency was necessary because Jon expected a job offer from a local school district within the week. While the school district took its time, we brought in Jon and — without skipping a step — completed our interview process within a matter of days and offered him the job. No matter who else was in our hiring process, we didn't want to miss out on a great hire. Since then, Jon has advanced to a leadership position in our company. Boy, would my company have been disadvantaged if we'd dragged our feet to compare Jon with another candidate!

11. **Don't predetermine how much your company is willing to pay a candidate to fill your open position. Pay whatever it takes to hire a candidate who will provide bench strength and achieve your company goals.** Predetermining a salary cap can cause your company to miss out on hiring "the ablest, most earnest, and reliable in the field of business." After interviewing, determine if the candidate's salary expectations are realistic and reasonable. You have to be able to cover the expense, of course. But don't cheap out if the person will provide bench strength and achieve your company goals.

When we needed to hire an accountant, we could have saved money by hiring a low-wage bookkeeper or recent trade school graduate. Instead, we hired Mike, who had worked as a controller and assistant controller during his 25-year career. For a guy of that caliber, you don't pay entry-level wages. And, more importantly, you don't get entry-level performance. Mike proved to be excellent in his core duties and provided additional value by helping us develop a cash forecast and install a complicated software program that affected almost our entire business. And rather than asking us questions like most new hires, Mike taught us about general business best practices, HR/benefits, and unemployment. If we had capped the amount we were willing to pay an accountant, we'd have missed out on all the great things Mike provided our company. Looking back, it was money well spent.

12. **Don't hire kids just out of college.** Here's another rule of thumb that might make you gasp. *Everybody* hires at least *some* recent college grads, right? I'll talk about exceptions later, but hear me out on the merits of this rule:
    - Kids just out of college haven't built up the history that enables a prospective employer to accurately predict their long-term success at the job.
    - They bring with them no bank of real-world experience doing what you need done.
    - They won't be able to teach you anything or contribute more than their labor.
    - Training them to meet your standard requires more management labor than you should be willing to expend on one employee.

- Too large a percentage of your customers won't take a kid seriously. It will be several years before the new hire is regarded as a trusted consultant.
- Professional jobs are exponentially more difficult than college course work. Recent graduates typically struggle to make the adjustment from academia (12–15 class hours per week, long breaks throughout the year) to a real job (40+ hours per week every week, no long breaks).
- There is a high probability that a recent grad will quit any first employer to see if the grass is greener somewhere else. How many 30-somethings do you know who have held the same professional job since the day after they graduated from college? I'm guessing that number is fewer than 10. (And, as good-looking as you are, I bet you have *thousands* of acquaintances.) Play the percentages. Don't hire a kid fresh out of college if you want your new hire to grow your business.

Let's talk now about the type of recent grad you *should* consider hiring. Tim joined our team right after he finished college, and he's been a key contributor ever since. Almost every other recent graduate we hired has quit because, like pretty much everyone else on the planet, their life circumstances changed significantly between the ages of 22 and 32. So how was Tim different? First, he had real responsibilities — a fiancée and young child. That meant Tim had real-world experience that most kids don't have. While going to school, he worked a full-time job to support his family. So while a 40-hour workweek is usually two or three times more effort than a college kid is used to giving, for Tim it was a respite from tests, tasks, and a teething toddler. When we asked for examples during our interviews, Tim provided them in great detail. He was uncommonly mature — a character trait atypical in kids who have recently surpassed the legal drinking age. Tim has continued to mature at Jameson, moving from sales training to sales to a successful run as a sales manager for a multi-million dollar product group.

13. **Don't beg a candidate to take your job.** If the candidate believes they're doing you a favor by taking your job, the probability is that your employment relationship will be rocky. You will need to continue to beg that person to perform the job. My company hasn't broken this rule, so I don't have an example to support this rule of thumb. And I won't give you an example even if you beg.

14. **Don't hire smokers.** (Note: This rule of thumb might not be legal in some states — especially those along Tobacco Road.) This is another rule of thumb that raises eyebrows, but every non-smoker with whom I've talked it through sees the wisdom in it. The only folks who disagree are, predictably, some smokers. It is almost a certainty that a regular tobacco habit will diminish smokers' productivity, depreciate your real estate, annoy their non-smoking co-workers, and damage employee-manager relationships. Plus, managing this issue adds an unnecessary level of grief and liability to your business.

My first summer job was in the employee services department at the Erie Zoological Gardens. (You might think everybody who works at a zoo shovels elephant poop all day long, but that's not the case. I worked in the concession stands, ticket booth, carousel, and other areas where employees interacted with visitors. I smelled lots of elephant poop but never touched the stuff.) My last year on the job was the summer after my freshman year in college. A new hiring manager had brought in a wave of new high schoolers, some of them smokers. The previous hiring manager never hired smokers, so this was my first exposure to nicotine-addicted team members. I learned firsthand that their habit will harm:

- *Their productivity:* After we'd served a flurry of customers on busy days, the concession stand needed all hands on deck to wipe the counters, refill the ketchup dispensers, and fill the napkin holders before the next wave hit. But the smokers needed a quick hit. So they'd leave the concession stand to smoke in the employee break room, which meant the size of the clean-up crew was cut in half.
- *Your real estate:* Our break room was already crummier than the monkey cages, but the smokers made it intolerable. When I punched out for lunch, I'd have to walk through a smoke-filled hallway. When the smokers weren't taking a(nother) break, the room was a mess because they tossed their cigarette butts on the floor.
- *The attitude of non-smoking co-workers:* Based on what you've just read, how do you think I felt about my smoking teammates? When we needed helping hands, they weren't there. They trashed the break room. And they were belligerent when asked to change their behavior. "It's a habit," was their excuse. I told them playing basketball was my habit. So would they mind if I took a break during a rush of customers to dribble around the giraffe exhibit? They argued that their habit was excusable because it was an addiction. I'm sure my employer enjoyed paying us for having these conversations.

- *Employee-manager relationships:* The veteran employees tasked with training the new-hire smokers resented the extra grief they had to endure. *Where's Steph? She's been gone for 20 minutes now. You just had your hands near your mouth. Wash your hands before touching the food. You've already taken three breaks today. Do you really need another?*

Hiring casual smokers is acceptable, but there are very few true casual smokers. Candidates often smoke more than they claim they do.

15. **Don't hire someone who is in the midst of a disruptive life crisis.** I haven't hired anyone who referred in an interview to being at a crossroads. This could be as benign as uncertainty about long-term living arrangements *(I'm really tired of living in a cold climate. Maybe I'll move to North Carolina, where my sister lives.)* or career indecision *(I don't know if I want to stay in sales.)*. A disruptive life crisis could also include separation, divorce, or other legal disputes. Separation and divorce are among the most disturbing and disruptive — sometimes devastating — life events. Odds are, your company will not receive 40 hours' work for 40 hours' pay until six months or a year after the divorce is final. Candidates whose circumstances are in such flux can't accurately predict where they will be or what they'll be doing in the future. The only people who argue this rule of thumb have never been close to someone who has gone through a divorce.

We've followed this best practice and told candidates we won't hire them at a time when their life is filled with so much uncertainty. At the moment, they argue that's not the case. But when we later bump into them or an acquaintance of theirs, we learn they've moved out of town and/or started a different career that better fit their new lifestyle.

16. **When hiring for a supervisory or leadership position, hire someone willing to start in a lower-level position.** Without a deep, rich understanding of your company culture, new hires will need to learn how to treat others and how to defend what's important to the company. This allows you to train and test employees — at a stage when their mistakes can be more easily managed and corrected — before delegating higher-impact responsibilities to them. In the past, my company placed new hires directly into management/leadership positions. That resulted in managers who lacked a deep understanding of their

direct reports, their direct reports' duties, and our company culture. Because they did not fully understand our best practices or the situation, new-hire managers made poor decisions that frustrated direct reports who were already skeptical of an unproven manager.

This extended training process will require your company to anticipate hiring needs sooner or tolerate a greater workload until the new hires are up to speed and can move into the long-term positions they were hired to fill.

When you ask questions to get a full understanding of the situation and the candidate's circumstances, you may often find that the rule of thumb does not apply. (Repeated for emphasis.) Exceptions to these guidelines must be based on fact. Don't disregard a rule because it makes your job more difficult or because you don't understand its value. (Also repeated for emphasis.)

Although these *Hiring Rules of Thumb* are stated as absolutes, the hiring manager must apply critical thinking and discernment to make the best decision. Do not shut off your brain!

PART II

Decision-Making & Communication Skills

As previously noted, the purpose of your pre-employment interviews is to determine if the candidate is a good match for your company in terms of skills, personality, character, and mapping. To achieve this outcome, the hiring manager needs to communicate effectively with the candidate.

Because communication is dynamic, you will hear many different responses from candidates. Making critical thinking part of pre-interview preparation enables the hiring manager to react to whatever information the candidate presents. These decision-making and communication skills are the bridge between the guiding principles we've already outlined and the execution of the pre-employment process.

Bottom line: A hiring manager who excels at these skills will excel at pre-employment interviewing and decision-making. A hiring manager deficient in any of these skills must improve in order to make appropriate pre-employment decisions.

CHAPTER 7

Decision-Making Skills

Critical Thinking

*C*ritical Thinking is the process of determining what you want to accomplish (the outcome), evaluating what you know, and determining what actions must be taken to achieve that outcome. A hiring manager who thinks critically will be able to analyze complex situations your company's policies may not specifically address. Your company and this book can document the steps required to solve some core pre-employment problems. But these documents alone will not be completely effective because:

- Especially for complex issues, documented objectives cannot be detailed enough to match specific situations.
- The best-practice procedures will be abandoned because the employees executing the hiring process do not understand how the procedures can help them achieve their desired outcomes.
- Those employees are not even thinking of the outcome, because their attention is diverted away from outcomes by tasks they're required to perform.

Here are the six basic steps of Critical Thinking for pre-employment interviews:

1. Fully understand the philosophy and process of the best practices, such as the principles outlined in this book and current HR law.

2. <u>Fully understand the situation.</u> What is the target of your interview process? What company need are you trying to fill? What are the target skills, personality, character, and mapping traits for the new hire? Once you've answered those questions, thoroughly review the candidate's pre-employment tests, résumé, answers to previous questions, observations and opinions of others on your interview team, and whatever other information has been gathered. You can't conduct the interview process in a vacuum.

3. <u>Clearly define the desired outcomes for the interview.</u> Determine the business and emotional outcomes you want to achieve. If those concepts are unclear to you, you haven't read the previous seven chapters closely enough. Go back to Chapter 1 and start again. Do not pass "Go." Do not collect $200.

4. <u>Detail your action plan.</u> Review the questions in the back of this book to determine which questions you will ask to achieve your outcomes. Create your own questions, too.

5. <u>Evaluate your plan.</u> Review your action plan in the order it will probably be executed. Obviate how the candidate may respond to your questions. Ask yourself if this plan will achieve your intended outcomes. Adjust your plan as needed.

6. <u>Develop a contingency plan.</u> Assume that parts of your original plan won't work. What will you do if the plan does not achieve the desired outcome? Develop follow-up questions to answers the candidate might give. Prepare questions to ask if the candidate responds differently than you anticipate. And again ask yourself, "Will this plan achieve my intended outcomes?"

Now let's apply those six steps to the real world. I currently interview only candidates who have passed our pre-employment tests and interviewed twice with someone from our HR department, who has listed for me observations of the candidate and potential aversions. Then it's time for me to put on my critical-thinking cap.

1. <u>Fully understand the philosophy and process of the best practices:</u> When I was a new hiring manager, I partnered with a more experienced hiring manager to learn the best practices. After several years of conducting interviews and keeping up to speed with current HR law, this step is essentially now a non-event for me.

2. <u>Fully understand the situation:</u> First I review the résumé to get my bearings: where the candidate lives and attended school, current and past employment. I then get the skinny from my co-worker(s) who conducted the initial interviews. Instead of reviewing every question they asked the candidate, we start by talking through their aversions. I pepper them with questions to help me fully understand the candidate and specific aversions. You can't assume one candidate's aversions are equal to another's. The aversion of *long talker* could mean the candidate adds a few extra words to each answer, which is occasionally annoying. Or it could mean the candidate frequently steers the conversation off path and misses the point of the question. That aversion is more than an annoyance. It's a potential deal-breaker.

   I then spend up to a half-hour at my desk, reading every detail of the paperwork related to the candidate. If I can't find answers to my questions, I make a note to remind myself to obtain that info during our interview. I also look through the paperwork to identify new potential aversions to talk about. Finally, I reread our company's hiring targets for the available position to see how the candidate aligns (or doesn't align) with them.

3. <u>Clearly define the desired outcomes for the interview:</u> Emotional outcomes don't vary greatly from candidate to candidate. Business outcomes are a different story. If I join the interview process halfway through, I basically focus on the top aversions. I'll gather an avalanche of information on them and test whether the candidate meets our target. My goal is to leave the interview with all the data I need to make a decision on those key aversions. I'm always looking for new aversions, but my primary outcomes are related to aversions we've already uncovered.

4. <u>Detail your action plan:</u> This part isn't very flashy. I power up my laptop, open a blank page in Microsoft Word, and type questions for each aversion. Some of the questions I'll ask are already on my company's list of standard interview questions. Some have been asked in the previous interviews, but I plan to ask them again with a slightly different angle. And some questions I create on my own. I group my questions by aversion, knowing that if I ask them all with appropriate follow-ups, I will achieve my business outcomes. From a formatting perspective, I leave just over an inch of space after each question so I have room to write the candidate's answers during our interview.

5. <u>Evaluate your plan:</u> I'm not a believer in the paperless office, so I always print my questions and read the hard copy. I ask myself if I think these questions flow the way I want and if they'll achieve the outcomes I'm looking for. Sometimes I'll even read the questions out loud to see if they sound right instead of just reading well. I also walk my questions over to the co-worker(s) who conducted the previous interviews to get their take on my plan. They'll often predict how the candidate might answer, so we'll talk through potential follow-up questions we can ask in the interview.

6. <u>Develop a contingency plan:</u> I'll imagine myself in the candidate's shoes and test how I'd answer my own questions. Could I spin an answer to make myself look good? What follow-up questions would I ask to cut through the smoke screen and get the real answer? I also think about how my best co-workers and some of our failed hires would answer. I learn how deep I'll probably need to dig beyond surface answers to find the truth.

Critical Thinking is so vital to your interview process that I'm going to take this explanation one step further and share my raw planning notes from one particular interview. The HR folks who conducted the initial interviews had two main aversions about Trudy, an editor candidate. First, during her 20-year career, Trudy had either worked in academia or been self-employed and worked from home. Could she adapt to our office environment, which required teamwork and pointed conversations with co-workers? And even if she could adapt, would she enjoy that environment so much that she'd never go back to self-employment or the academic world? Second, Trudy didn't seem to have as outgoing a personality as we hoped for in an editor. Would she be comfortable meeting with customers at trade shows, working the room at a reception, and making a presentation to hundreds of attendees?

Here was my plan to gather data on each aversion without revealing the aversion to Trudy. Keep in mind these are my raw notes based on her information packet. Some questions are notes for myself to prompt me to press a particular angle if I need to:

Academia vs. Professional Publishing Company Office vs. Self-Employed

Where are you now in your job search? Are you actively looking? If so, what other types of companies/positions have you looked at or applied to? Marketing? Sales?

Why does she want to join a team now?

Wants $40k to start. Why does she want only $40k after 20 years in the workforce? Find out why she's tolerated low pay. Will she bail if the job gets tough because she doesn't need the money?

What are the most difficult things about your current job? Do the core "cons" of that job match the core "cons" of our editor job?

Said she likes our company's structure like starting work time, scheduled lunch time. Why does she want that structure now?

Give me an example of a criticism you've received. How did it help you or how did you react? Get all 4 angles – valuable criticism you followed, valuable criticism you didn't follow, invalid criticism you followed, invalid criticism you didn't follow. How does she handle various forms of criticism?

Give me examples of times when you had to do the hard thing or have a difficult conversation. Give me an example of you doing it well, then an example of doing it not well. Get 2 examples for each.

How do you feel about the policies and procedures used by the company you work for now? Too many? Too few? Does she feel stifled by policies/systems that are similar to ours?

Tell me how you felt about your last supervisor in terms of fairness and competence. Dig to learn if it was close supervision. Ask about other supervisors — find out if they were close managers.

What would your previous employers say are your strengths and weaknesses? Was she actually exposed to this through performance reviews or is she guessing?

Do you agree? If not, what would *you* say are your strengths and weaknesses?

What's the last thing on which you and your boss disagreed? How did you settle it? Get 2 examples.

Describe an unpleasant work situation in the past and tell me how you dealt with it. Get 2 examples.

Give me an example of a time when you weren't getting along with a co-worker. How did you get it resolved? Get 2 examples.

Tell me about how you dealt with an angry or frustrated customer. Was she exposed to customers or insulated from them — did she get her hands dirty with customers?

How do you feel about our company in terms of its size and industry? Why? Which past jobs did she prefer — larger or smaller? School or self-employment? Get specific comparison/contrast of these jobs.

What tasks do you find most stimulating or interesting? What tasks do you like the least?

What things are you looking for in a job? What is your ideal job?

Personality — has she/does she incline toward people interaction?

What showed up in her answer to "What tasks do you find most stimulating or interesting? What tasks do you like the least?"

What showed up in her answer to "What things are you looking for in a job? What is your ideal job?"

Have you ever worked with salespeople? Tell me about a problem you've had in the past with a co-worker in sales. How did you solve it? Get 2 examples.

How does she feel about working with salespeople?

Does she have examples of executing a sales/marketing plan in her business? Get example of a successful plan and an unsuccessful plan. Did she enjoy developing/executing the plan? Did she include personal contact or was it all mail/email? Why?

Where do you fit the following in the interesting/least interesting categories: public speaking, working a cocktail party, trade show appointments, 1-on-1 interviews, TV appearances, radio interviews. Rank them along with other tasks. Get examples if she's done these before.

Skepticism & Validation

Skepticism is an attitude of doubt. It's basically saying, "I'm not sure if I can believe you," but it's expressed in a way that shouldn't be as blunt as that. *Validation* confirms or refutes your skepticism. Hiring managers are supposed to be skeptical. They must seek all the facts. Hold out for specific facts, as opposed to words conveying feelings or vague explanation.

- Skepticism ensures that hiring managers operate on facts and truths. This enables them and your company to make the right choices and moves. Conversely, you won't achieve desired results if you don't operate on facts and truths. And you will waste company time and money.

- Skepticism allows a hiring manager to obtain as much information as possible in order to make the best possible choice or take the best possible action.

- Skepticism helps the hiring manager gain enough facts to make an answer clear.

- Humans, in general, will stretch the truth, ignore certain facts, or cover up others in an attempt to cast themselves in a favorable light. (That might sound cynical, but it's true. If you don't believe me, ask a middle-aged woman how much she weighs or ask a young man how much he bench presses.)

Avoid giving undue credit or casting undeserved blame. One instance of a specific attitude or behavior does not constitute a trend. Do not assume proficiency in any area until a candidate has given you multiple examples or passed several one-for-one tests (defined in the Glossary). Do not finalize your opinion of the candidate on the basis of one or two data points. Don't make the mistake of filling in the blanks with your assumptions. Instead, ask probing questions that will help you fully understand the reasons for the candidate's behavior in specific situations.

Ask follow-up questions that thoroughly drill down to get a full understanding. In the back of this book, you'll find initial questions for the topic you're exploring. Follow-up questions such as *Why?* and *Can you give me a specific example?* plus *Can you give me another example?* will help you obtain the true answer.

As a candidate provides answers or information surrounding a topic or situation, continually ask yourself:

- Do I have the full story?
- Do I need to know more?
- Do I believe what is being presented?
- What holes can I poke in this?

Do not reveal your skepticism. Ask all your questions in a friendly, non-threatening manner. Avoid saying "I don't believe you." Make it clear that you're on the candidate's side. Palatable ways to question candidates include such language as *That's great if that's the case … Can you help me understand … I'd like to get some more details from you on that …* and *Can you explain this aspect to me?* To prevent candidates from censoring subsequent answers, do not show disapproval or displeasure with their initial answers.

Near the end of your pre-employment process, examine sources of data such as reference checks, background checks, salary history, Internet and social media searches, and education/degree validation compared with what you *think* you know about a candidate. This will help you confirm what you *actually* know and could suggest additional questions.

CHAPTER 8

Communication Skills

QACF

No, *QACF* is not the sound a duck makes when it's trying to quack and eat at the same time. QACF is an acronym that represents the pattern your interview discussion should follow: Question, Answer, Comment, Feedback. You ask a question. The candidate answers. You make a related comment, then ask/wait for feedback. This makes the interview conversational and keeps candidates from feeling like they're being grilled or run through a survey.

More specifically:

- **Q & A** is the process by which you ask a clear, succinct, probing question and the candidate answers it (information gathering). Q doesn't always have to be a question. It can be a request or statement.
- **C** is when you comment in response to the candidate's answer. The comment validates your understanding of the answer.
- **F** is when the candidate provides feedback that typically affirms or disputes that you understood the original answer.

A candidate won't want to interact with a hiring manager whose continuous questioning creates a confrontational relationship. But you may occasionally want to follow the QAQAQAQAQA pattern to test how candidates handle confrontation, whether they mirror you, or if they keep their cool.

A good strategy to follow in order to learn the truth is to paraphrase the candidate's response to your question. It shows that you are listening. (QACF, QAQAQAQAQACF, QAQAQACF, etc.)

Example:
> Tell me about a time you had to confront a co-worker you worked with on a regular basis.
> *The candidate answers.*
> Why did you use that tactic?
> *The candidate answers.*
> How did the situation make you feel?
> *The candidate answers.*
> If you had to do it again, what would you do differently?
> *The candidate answers.*
> Interesting that you say that. A lot of people struggle with a new co-worker who was added to their team without much warning. But it seems like you and this co-worker are on good terms now.
> *The candidate provides feedback on your comment.*

Here are six tips for effective use of QACF:

1. Listen to candidates' answers and react naturally to their cues.
2. Don't assume anything.
3. Let candidates fully answer your questions. Don't interrupt. Take notes to capture pertinent points that you want to come back to later in the conversation.
4. Engage candidates. Talk about *their* experiences, not yours.
5. Have a good understanding of your questions. Prepare your questions in advance so you don't fumble your way through the conversation.
6. Listen! Your Q and C should be succinct. The candidate's A and F should be more detailed.

Getting Specifics

Getting Specifics is directly connected with *Skepticism & Validation* (previous chapter). Good decisions can be made only if the facts are known; facts live in specifics, not generalities. Competent hiring managers will make good choices when faced with all the facts. But most of us won't make the effort required to obtain all the facts. A candidate who does not want to get to the truth will give vague answers to prevent the truth being known. Getting Specifics eliminates the candidate's ability to mask the truth.

By removing any presumption, Getting Specifics also builds rapport and respect between the hiring manager and the candidate. The hiring manager doesn't presume to know it all and needs the candidate's input to make the correct decision. Open-ended questions are preferred because they leave room for any answer. This prevents the candidate from feeling backed into a corner by your questions. Plus you'll get more detail, especially when an answer isn't clear or simple.

Remain skeptical until you receive proof or validate the truth of any answer. Ask deeper questions, based on the candidate's answers, to draw out all the information. Get specific factual details — times, dates, names, places, order of events, etc. — until you confirm a trend. Many people are good at talking around a subject without divulging the fact that they never actually accomplished anything.

Follow up your questions with requests for specific examples. If an example isn't specific enough, stop the candidate and explain that you want such details as order of events, first names, and paraphrases of what was said.

Repeat the Question

Repeating the Question ensures that you receive an answer to the question you asked. If you don't use this technique, you let candidates off the hook and you may not get the answers you need.

Instead of repeating a question that hasn't been fully answered, the hiring manager often moves on to the next question. This allows the candidate to evade the original question. If you allow candidates to evade difficult questions and you're not able to get a full understanding of their situation, you have little hope of getting the data needed to make accurate hiring decisions.

About 12 years into my career at Jameson, I conducted only the Dinner Interview and Final Aversions Interview of our rigorous process. Other managers had conducted the first rounds of interviews with Kerry, the sales candidate I was tasked with interviewing. Despite being a veteran sales rep, mentor, and manager, Kerry had provided weak answers to the question *What do you consider your top five accomplishments in life?* (As an example, one of her answers was "common sense.") When I reviewed her information packet prior to our interview, I was very concerned with her feeble answers to that question. There's a high likelihood we won't hire the person who doesn't give a good answer to that question, especially one who has several years' work experience. Why should we expect a candidate who hasn't accomplished anything with previous employers to suddenly start achieving greatness with our company?

So here's what I said to Kerry early in my interview with her: "I'd like to ask you a question again that you answered in a previous interview. The question was *What do you consider* your *top five accomplishments in life?* I've asked this question of a lot of people. And if I charted their answers on a spectrum from weakest to strongest, yours would be among the weakest. This is an important question because, as we've talked about already, initiative is a very important trait at our company. So I'd like you to try again to answer this question, but I'd like all your examples to be work-related. What do you consider your top five professional accomplishments? Feel free to take all the time you need."

Kerry was a little flustered. She had already spent several hours with our team and really wanted the job. She started answering the question, but her descriptions were vague. So as kindly as I could, I butted in. "Sorry to interrupt," I said. "I'm still not getting a clear picture of your accomplishments. Can you please provide me with as many specifics as you can? What specifically did you accomplish?" Kerry said, "OK," then painted a vivid description of being named employee of the month at her previous employer because a program she initiated increased her entire department's sales. That answer was exactly what I was looking for, so I told her that. "That's one," I said. "I'd love to hear four more like that." I still wasn't done repeating the question, however. When Kerry finished her list of accomplishments, I pointed out that one was related to college, not work, and asked her to give me one more professional accomplishment, which she did.

That was an example of Repeating the Question to draw out necessary information. You can also use this communication technique to get to the truth when a candidate's initial answer intentionally avoids telling the whole story.

Rolling Why

Remember when skater Tonya Harding and her boyfriend Jeff Gillooly conspired to whack Nancy Kerrigan on the leg so she couldn't compete in the 1994 Olympic figure skating trials? The whole saga was regrettable from every angle. What I recall most vividly was Kerrigan writhing in pain after being hit on the knee, repeatedly screaming *Why? Why? Why?* Nancy was asking that question in a moment of despair, but hiring managers should be asking that question to candidates throughout the interview process. If this were a conversation instead of a book, I'd be raising my voice here: *Why?* is <u>the</u> best question you can ask a candidate.

The Rolling Why consists of asking *Why?* continually until you gain that deep understanding of the purpose of the candidate's action or thinking. We often make false assumptions, filling in the blanks based on what could be erroneous information. A frequent *Why?* will ensure that you learn all the candidate knows concerning the subject.

Answers to these questions generally reveal more data on the specific subject. But they could also lead to another subject. Example: A hiring manager applies the Rolling Why to *Why are you leaving your current job?* If the answer is *I'm not getting paid enough,* the Rolling Why *(Why? Why else?)* could elicit details about the candidate's pay, its unfairness, or the company's dismal future. But it could also lead to claims that management is unreasonable, take you into conflicts this person has with management, and expose an aversion that the candidate has problems with supervision.

Here are four tips for executing the Rolling Why:

1. Be sure you don't sound like a broken record, asking Why? in a serial fashion. Mix in other questions and comments.
2. When you don't understand an answer, ask *Why?* directly or rephrase in the form of a full question. Examples: *Could you help me understand the reason you did that? Why did you do that? Why is that important to you? Why do you think that approach worked?*
3. Be sure your questions are connected to an outcome. Don't ask *Why?* just because you can't think of another question.
4. Integrate *Why?* when developing your line of interview questions.

So when you're preparing for your next interview … think Nancy Kerrigan.

The 90:10 Ratio & the 30-Second Rule

We've talked quite a bit about asking questions, but you're not going to hear any data from the candidate unless you zip it occasionally. Follow *The 90:10 Ratio.* The candidate should talk at least 90% of the time; you should talk, at most, 10% of the time.

- Listen to each answer in full. Do not anticipate what the candidate is going to say.
- When the candidate stops talking, nod your head — a non-verbal suggestion to continue talking.

When you don't talk, the candidate doesn't know what you're thinking and often will start talking to fill the silence. This helps you gain more information and, when appropriate, can defuse a confrontational situation.

Will some of the silence be awkward? Yep. But use it to your advantage. Don't speak just because the silence becomes uncomfortable for *you*. Silence — even uncomfortable silence — can be beneficial if you want to:

- Encourage the candidate to talk more on the subject.
- See how the candidate reacts to pressure.
- Test the candidate's ability to stay silent.
- Take some time to think.
- Take additional notes.
- Maintain emotional control.
- Change the mood of the meeting from casual/fun to serious.

Additionally, silence prevents the hiring manager from leading the candidate to an answer. This forces the candidate to respond. In other words, wait as long as it takes to get an answer from the candidate.

Lengthy questions or comments can undermine your ability to gain information. *The 30-Second Rule* is a guideline that you should talk for 30 seconds or less each time you speak. Otherwise, you jeopardize the effectiveness of the discussion. The 30-Second Rule improves communication and understanding between the hiring manager and the candidate because it separates individual points, making them easier to digest and understand even in long, in-depth conversations. If you talk longer than 30 seconds at a time, you increase the likelihood that the candidate will miss your point. This rule doesn't always literally mean 30 seconds, but it conveys a clear and memorable communication principle that you need to control your conversation with a candidate.

A few years back, I interviewed with a local high school basketball coach about me possibly coaching his program's freshman team. I had several questions about the demands and expectations of the job, and I figured he'd want to learn about me. He welcomed me into his office, leaned back in the chair behind his desk, and launched a half-hour verbal retrospective of his basketball career. I squeezed in a couple questions about things I needed to know, but quickly realized this guy wasn't a fit for me. He concluded the conversation by saying he'd love to have me be a part of his program and thought I could do a good job. I thought to myself, "Based on what data? My haircut? My posture? My freckles?" He hadn't learned a thing about me, except that I was a patient listener.

To use the 30-Second Rule effectively, provide small pieces of information on the message you're trying to convey to the candidate. Follow up by asking a question or asking for feedback. Communication improves because you actively engage the candidate in the conversation. While more complex topics require more explanation, the information will be more easily understood if you stop and ask for feedback during the explanation. Resist the tendency to keep talking until you exhaust the subject.

Last Presented Issue

A *Last Presented Issue* is the most recent problem (commonly an attitude) that a candidate has presented and that must be made the focus of attention before the original issue can be effectively addressed. Typical Last Presented Issue attitudes include:

1. Combativeness
2. Resistance
3. Deflection
4. Acquiescence
5. Passive-aggressiveness
6. Lack of sincerity

If the candidate's inappropriate attitude detracts from addressing the original issue, suspend discussion and address the attitude. Once the Last Presented Issue is resolved, refocus on the original issue.

One of our company's hiring managers ran headfirst into a Last Presented Issue with a sales candidate who happened to be a 6' 5", 250-pound former college athlete we'll call Mike. You'll understand later why I mention Mike's imposing appearance. Mike had answered our initial questions in laid-back fashion such as *I get along with all my co-workers* and *My manager and I get along really well.*

Wanting to expose Mike to an aversion, our hiring manager said, "You said you were OK with criticism. So can I share one with you?" The hiring manager pointed out several instances during the interview when Mike strayed from the path of the conversation and provided unnecessary details. Basically, he told Mike he was a long talker, an issue which sales reps and sales managers need to correct in order to be effective. As the hiring manager delivered this message, Mike's smile became a scowl and his face turned beet red. He leaned forward on the conference room table and curled his hands into fists. His loud reaction included such comments as *Who do you think you are?* and *I've never been so insulted in my life!*

The Last Presented Issue was Mike's combativeness and loss of emotional control. The hiring manager had to address it. He couldn't just respond in a chipper voice, "That answer was more succinct than others you've given. Good job, Mikey!" He had to stop the conversation about long talking, directly address Mike's poor behavior, and dig into the areas of combativeness and loss of emotional control. If Mike could overcome those problems, they could get back to long talking. As you might imagine, Mike didn't change his attitude, so we didn't hire him.

Be alert to multiple attitudes presenting. You may have to take two or three steps beyond the original issue. Follow the candidate, identifying and address-ing each attitude along the way. If the candidate continues to present multiple attitudes, you must at some point refer to the amount of time being wasted by having to address Last Presented Issues.

Combining Empathy With Aggressiveness

This concept should be integrated into every candidate interaction. The more aggressive you become, the more empathetic you must be.

Aggressiveness is not harsh. It is simply persistence in getting the information you need to make a good hiring decision and clearly communicating your per-ceptions of the candidate's actual or potential aversions for the job and your company.

Empathy is not sympathy. It is understanding and valuing the candidate's feelings without losing sight of the best interests of your company and the individual.

Combining empathy with aggressiveness is important because it:

- Allows you to make clear-minded decisions that adhere to facts and truth while treating the candidate fairly. As a result, the decisions you make will be in the candidate's best interest <u>and</u> your company's best interest.
- Makes candidates feel you are helping them with their struggles, not attacking their weaknesses.
- Helps achieve your emotional outcomes.

Let me try to clarify this principle by sharing an example that involved a sales candidate at my company. (I shared portions of this example in *Repeat the Question*. So if anything sounds familiar, you're not losing your mind.) I was involved at the end of Kerry's interview process, which means I reviewed her interview packet, talked about her in detail with the hiring manager, and first met her for a Dinner Interview (the penultimate step in our hiring process). The data and our interactions showed me that Kerry was a pleasant person and wouldn't be a bad hire, but I wasn't sure if she had the potential to be an *excellent* hire. That was what we were shooting for, and what you should be shooting for.

When Kerry came to our office for the Final Aversions Interview, I had to combine empathy with aggressiveness to achieve my goals. Let me break down the conversation into those two categories:

Empathy: "I know you've spent a lot of time with us, and you are probably thinking you have a really good chance at getting this job. That's true. If we were going to spend today listing all your good qualities, we'd be here for the next several hours."

Aggressiveness: "But I don't have data that says you'll take initiative to solve a problem, and I don't have evidence your actions at past jobs have generated impressive, concrete results."

Empathy: "I'm going to give you a chance to prove to us that you have those qualities. I'd like to ask you a question that you answered in a previous interview. The question is: *What do you consider your top five accomplishments in life?*"

Aggressiveness: "I've asked this question of a lot of people, and if I charted all their answers on a spectrum from weakest to strongest, yours would be among the weakest. This is an important question because, as we've talked about already, initiative is a very important trait at our company. So I'd like you to try again to answer this question, but I'd like all your examples to be work-related. What do you consider your top five professional accomplishments?"

Empathy: "Feel free to take all the time you need."

We spent about a half-hour on this subject, with Kerry doing almost all the talking. But I frequently interjected, and balanced empathy and aggressiveness.

Empathy, then Aggressiveness: "Sorry to interrupt. I'm still not getting a clear picture of your accomplishments. Can you please provide me with as many specifics as you can? What specifically did you accomplish?"

Empathy: "That's one. I'd love to hear four more like that."

Empathy, then Aggressiveness: "Four of those five were just what I was looking for. But the last one wasn't strong. Plus, it was an example from school, not work. So can you replace that with another work-related accomplishment?"

I questioned Kerry for another hour. Before turning the interview back over to the hiring manager, I gave Kerry one more dose of empathy. "Sorry if I came off as harsh," I said. "I was just trying to make sure this is a right fit for you and for us."

Kerry replied with some empathy and aggressiveness for me. "That's fine. Those were fair questions," she said. "Did you get the data you needed?" When I responded that I did, she closed by asking, "Are you ready to hire me?" We made Kerry an offer the next day, and she gladly accepted.

Set Them Up For Future Reference

If you can master *Set Them Up For Future Reference,* you'll hire the right candidate and begin the new hire on the right management path. This communication technique — I convert it to the fun acronym STUFFR — consists of identifying and understanding a potential problem and discussing it with the candidate in advance. You also need to note the candidate's (and your own) exact words and commitment to not failing. In a cheerful, non-threatening way, I let candidates know that I'm writing their words in ink. So they better be certain before they comment, because I can't erase ink. They don't feel pressured, but they know I'm taking their words seriously.

Two important benefits of STUFFR are rapid improvement in deficient areas and accountability:

1. Most people want to make their word good and will improve below-standard performance faster after they make a commitment to do so. People feel obligated to live up to their word.

2. If candidates don't live up to their word after you hire them, you can play back the words they committed to in the interview. Arguing with your own words is tough to do. Employees usually acknowledge, apologize, and function up quickly.

Here's the four-step process for STUFFR:

1. Obviate. This means to anticipate and prevent. A simple form of obviating is looking out your window, noting the gray skies, and grabbing an umbrella in case of rain. You don't have to see raindrops to anticipate that you might get drenched later. Obviating requires skepticism. You need to look at your workplace situation (your company culture and the job requirements, for example) and the candidate's situation (such as their personality and experience) and discuss what could go wrong and what the two of you can do to prevent it.

2. Set clear expectations. Don't just say to a sales candidate, "We need you to work super hard — pound the pavement and pound the phone." Say more specifically, "After you complete our 6-week training program, you'll be required to have at least 10 face-to-face appointments each week and 10 phone contacts with potential customers. Those are the minimum productivity requirements. Sales reps who can't meet those numbers each week can't have this job."

3. Recap the conversation to ensure that you both agree. You could recap the previous conversation by saying, "So you're OK signing up for a job that requires 10 in-person appointments and 10 phone contacts each week? You won't be back in this room a month or a year after you finish training, saying those targets are too high?"

4. Write it down! Don't rely on your memory to capture details of your discussion. Make notes during the interview and file them with the candidate's other pre-employment documents. Again using the previous example, you could hire a sales candidate who later missed their productivity goals by a mile. When you sit down to discuss the 10-a-week minimums, the sales rep could claim, "You didn't say 10 a *week*. You said 10 a *month*." If you don't have clear notes, your best response will be "Nuh-uh!" Or you could start doubting yourself: Did you maybe slip up and say 10 a month? If you properly STUFFR and made good notes, all you need to do is open up the interview file and show the candidate details of the conversation. Management crisis averted.

Among the areas that my company Sets Them (candidates) Up For Future Reference:

- Work hours. We detail their specific start and end times, the consequences of not being on time, and manage candidates' expectations about the amount of overtime they can expect to work.
- The amount of paid leave time they'll start with.
- Starting pay and potential future pay.
- Productivity minimums.
- Travel expectations.
- Our company's cost-side-down philosophy. We expect all employees to be frugal (not wasteful) and look for ways to reduce expenses.
- Public displays of negative emotion. We don't tolerate screaming or tantrums. I actually say in the interview, "You're pretty much allowed to lose control twice. The first time, we'll sit down and I'll say, 'Remember in the interview process when we talked about how losing your temper is unacceptable behavior?' If we have to have a second conversation, we pretty much just get HR and help you clean out your desk."
- The potential strengths and pitfalls of the candidate's personality test. We also agree to meet regularly to ensure that potential weaknesses don't develop into debilitating problems.
- Improving weaknesses. We detail areas to improve and deliver a clear message that we will not tolerate ongoing below-standard performance. To have a successful career at our company, a candidate needs to exhibit continuous self-improvement and work within our principles and guidelines.

Most importantly, we STUFFR on our company culture, namely *The Golden Rule.* I don't care if someone generates a zillion dollars in new revenue. If that person doesn't treat co-workers right, I don't want that person on my team. Here's what I say: "You can take what I'm about to say to you two ways. You can take it as me wagging my finger in your face saying, 'We have a bunch of good, honest, kind, hard-working people here. Don't screw it up. I'll throw you out of here because I don't want one person ruining it for us.' Or you can take what I'm saying as our company making a commitment to you that you don't have to tolerate anyone screaming, yelling, swearing, or belittling you. If someone breaks the Golden Rule, let me know and we'll put a stop to it. Are you OK with that?"

So I'm setting the candidates and myself up for future reference. They know how they're required to behave, and they know we want them to report any shenanigans in our workplace. And they have my commitment that if they're being harmed, I'll do something about it.

PART III

Actionable Information

CHAPTER 9

Effective Recruiting Tactics

Over the years, my company has tested seemingly every recruiting tactic except having an HR employee walk around town wearing a "NOW HIRING" sandwich board. Our principle is that if the idea doesn't sound crazy, we test it to see if it works. And we add every one of our new recruiting efforts to our master list of recruiting activities, track the results, and briefly summarize whether it was worth our time. Referencing the activity list in recruiting brainstorming meetings jogs our memory to try a fruitful activity we haven't performed in a while. And if someone has what seems like a new idea, we check whether we've tested that activity and to gain perspective on how it worked.

Before we talk about building your list, let me share with you our list of best recruiting activities, listed from "Most Successful" to "Occasionally Successful." I've spared you the list that could be categorized "Well, That Was ___ Hours Of My Life I'll Never Get Back."

Referral Program

By far and away, our most successful recruiting activity has been our referral program. Referral programs won't yield as many résumés as an advertisement on employment websites, but the quality of candidates is far superior. Your employees — those who know your culture best — are your #1 source for finding candidates who fit your organization.

But you can't just announce "We've got a referral program" and then watch quality candidates line up. We've learned that successful referral programs need these four elements:

- A significant reward (e.g., $1,000 cash).
- Frequent communication.
- A passionate advocate/evangelist.
- Entertainment value.

This following example should paint a picture of how to execute a referral program:

On March 21, 2011, we called all our employees into our largest conference room for an announcement and ice cream. At our company, ice cream is more than just a treat; it lets everyone know we're not announcing bad news. Our HR director and I greeted employees as they entered the conference room and handed them a flyer with these details about our referral program:

Get Ready For The ...
Super 7 $777 Referral Contest!

If you refer a sales candidate, they complete a first interview between now and May 13, and we hire them in 2011, you will receive a $777 bonus. Among the qualities we prefer for sales:

- 2 or more years of successful proactive customer service experience
- Proven prospecting and closing ability
- Proven examples of hardiness and initiative
- Proven examples of resiliency/overcoming obstacles — bouncing back after getting knocked down
- Exemplifies our company principles

As you know, we've had success with candidates from all walks of life, so please refer people you know or folks you bump into who meet the above criteria. If your referral candidate doesn't have sales experience but is a real superstar in other ways, please talk with HR Director Ann Krugger.

Please email résumés to Ann.Krugger@JamesonPublishing.com. If you have questions, please call her at ext. 174.

The flyer included an image of a T-shirt featuring unicorns, rainbows, and the TV character Screech. (If you don't know Screech from "Saved by the

Bell," which aired in the early 1990s, you're really missing out.) Above that zany photo, which I found on the Internet, was this text: "Here's a suggestion for you if you earn the referral award. Not only does it cost less than $777, but you'd look FABULOUS in it. You probably own this awesome shirt already, but if you don't, your referral bonus can help you pay for a couple dozen of them!"

You'd think the $777 prize would get the most attention from our employees, but Screech stole the show. Before we started suggesting gag gifts in our referral program communications, nobody talked much about referrals. We'd distribute humdrum informational flyers, which most employees tossed aside when they got back to their desks. But for the Super 7 $777 Referral program, people actually hung the Screech flyer at their desks and talked about referrals even after the program ended.

The day after our group announcement, we scheduled a series of emails to be sent every two weeks or so to keep referrals top of mind. These brief messages mirrored the information and humor of the referral flyer:

Subject: Super 7 $777 Referral Contest Reminder & Fashion Suggestion

Friendly Reminder … If you refer a sales candidate, they complete a first interview between now and May 13, and we hire them in 2011, you will receive a $777 net bonus!

As you know, we've had success with candidates from all walks of life, so please refer people you think could be a good fit. Please send résumés to Ann.Krugger@JamesonPublishing.com. If you have questions, please call her at ext. 174.

ALSO … here's a fashion suggestion for you that costs less than $777 and would look FABULOUS on you (or a friend) this summer.

The emails featured such ridiculous images as flip-flops with stirrups attached, a woman wearing a ginormous sun hat, a T-shirt designed like a Christmas sweater, bright yellow pants with a multicolored flower pattern (my personal favorite), and a guy in a pink spandex shirt emblazoned with blue lightning bolts.

Silly? For sure. Effective? Absolutely. One of the referrals we received from this contest was hired and developed into an excellent addition to our sales team, making the $777 and the time we invested promoting the referral program totally worthwhile.

Our previous referral program included a $30 gift card for every candidate an employee referred. We discontinued that practice, mainly because the incentive was not aligned with our desired outcomes. All bonuses at our company are based on our goal to make employees feel the way the company feels. Well, an employee felt great about pocketing an extra $210 for referring seven candidates who made it to the interview stage. But the company didn't feel very good about interviewing seven referrals who didn't make the cut. In our new referral bonus program, the overall volume of referrals isn't as high, but the number of *quality* candidates is. We're achieving our hiring outcomes while spending less money and less overhead in HR labor.

I volunteer to be the referral program evangelist at our company. I strategize with our HR director on the contest theme and reward, send all the emails, field email replies from employees, and hype the program at our monthly company lunch. In addition to talking about the financial reward, I describe how important new hires are to our company's current needs and future growth.

I have a blast promoting our referral programs, especially this final step: After the new hire's first day, we call the referring employee and the new hire in front of the entire company and present a giant check to symbolize the bonus the referring employee has earned. We place Velcro on the back of the check so the employee can hang it up on their cube wall. It's a fun, year-round reminder of how important referrals are to our business and of the employee's contribution to our company.

Our most recent two-year analysis of effective recruiting methods showed that two-thirds of our new hires were referrals. If you don't have a referral program at your organization, launch one as soon as you can.

Job Fairs

We've hired employees from job fairs, but not always in the traditional manner. Of course, a qualified candidate may stop by your booth with résumé in hand. But some of the best candidates for your company may be on the *other* side of the table. Send at least two employees to every job fair — one to watch the booth and the other to walk booth to booth, engaging with exhibitors who could potentially join your team.

Start the conversation by introducing yourself as a fellow exhibitor, not a job seeker. Then ask about the exhibitor's company and that individual's role and career path. In three minutes, you've conducted a mini-job interview and probably have enough data to make the call to exchange business cards or move on to the next booth. On the back of every business card, note key points from your discussion. Because when you return to your desk after the job fair, the business cards you've collected will all blend together unless you distinguish them from each other. Within three business days, make follow-up phone calls to every potential hire you met at the job fair.

At one job fair my company attended, this "booth raid" technique produced two new hires currently in their second decade with our company. I'm surprised more companies don't utilize this effective technique.

Headhunters & Placement Agencies

My experience with headhunters has been hit and miss. Some really go to work for you and hunt down qualified candidates who weren't looking for a new job. Other firms take your information, send you anyone they have on file who could possibly be a fit, and cross their fingers you'll hire one of those candidates so they can make their sales quota.

My company engages in painstaking conversations with headhunter firms before we decide to work with them. We learn how successful they've been (or haven't been) hiring for companies and positions similar to ours. We share in great detail what we're looking for in a candidate. If a headhunter feels we're setting the bar too high, that's OK. We cross that firm off our list and don't waste more of anyone's time.

We also make sure the firm can meet our *Headhunter Contracting Guidelines* and is willing to comply with these five specifications:

1. Contingency Fee: My company signs performance-based headhunter contracts referred to in recruiting circles as *contingency searches*. If we do not hire an employee referred to us, we owe nothing, regardless of the effort or time the headhunter has expended. The alternative to a contingency headhunter is a *retained recruiter*. You pay a fee for the firm's effort, not results. Retained recruiting has not been a wise investment for my company.

2. <u>Minimum Three-Month Guarantee:</u> The contract must ensure that we receive a refund or the firm continues to search for us in the event that a referred employee leaves our company for any reason within three months of being hired. We try to negotiate up to six months with every headhunter. Some won't budge, but my company won't budge on anything less than a three-month guarantee.

3. <u>Rate Less Than 25%:</u> We won't sign a headhunter contract that requires us to pay a fee in excess of 25% of the new hire's first-year base salary. We've negotiated as low as 15% when our plan is to hire a high volume of employees, such as salespeople, through the headhunter. When you talk with a headhunter, understand that the rate is always negotiable. Don't accept the first percentage the headhunter offers you. If you make it clear that you are talking with several headhunters, the rate will suddenly become more competitive.

4. <u>Net 30 Payment Terms:</u> Fees in our headhunter contracts are payable Net 30 after the candidate begins working for us. Don't agree to pay for headhunter services as soon as the candidate agrees to work for you. You'll be in a pinch if you pay the bill and the candidate rescinds acceptance of your job offer. Every headhunter I've worked with has been amenable to this.

5. <u>Non-Solicitation:</u> We require assurance that the headhunter or any other member of that firm will not contact the referred employee, once hired, and will not present offers to any of our employees for at least two years from the point of engagement. The last thing you want to do is give a well-connected headhunter access to your talented team.

We hired about 10% of our employees through headhunter firms or employment agencies. Though that number seems low, consider that the time we invested in hiring these folks was minimal. We engaged only in interviewing activities, not recruiting. Good headhunters won't shovel a slew of unqualified candidates at your HR department. They will pinpoint candidates who merit your consideration.

People-Focused Website

I need you to do a little homework on my company's website before we talk about yours. The purpose of this exercise is for you to gain some perspective on the transition we've made from a product-focused site to a people-focused site:

1. Google "Internet Wayback Machine." This very cool site allows you to see websites as they appeared years ago.
2. In the box at the top of the page, enter www.CorryPub.com and click the Take Me Back button. Jameson Publishing's former name was Corry Publishing, and CorryPub.com was our Web address.
3. Click 2006 at the top of the page, then click on one of the highlighted dates on the calendar.
4. The Wayback Machine will show our company website before we revamped it to focus on attracting new employees rather than solely promote our products.
5. Now go to www.JamesonPublishing.com and check out its people-focused design.

Designed for prospective customers, our old site was all about our products. Our new and improved site still serves customers, but its main purpose is to inform and entice prospective candidates.

Implement these eight techniques to ensure that your website attracts candidates:

1. The home page should loudly promote your people and your company's achievements. Publishing Executive magazine lists Jameson Publishing among the "Best Magazine Publishing Companies To Work For" in the United States. To ensure that every candidate who visits our site knows we're a top employer, that honor commands a prominent spot on our home page. That placement works. One candidate mentioned to his buddies during a poker game that he was interviewing with us. His friend looked up our site the next day, called the candidate, and asked, "Did you realize you're interviewing with one of the best companies in America? Don't blow it!"

2. Don't make candidates jump through hoops to contact someone. From any page on our site, visitors can click Contact Us to obtain our phone number and office address. The Contact Us section also has a prominent Submit Résumé link; there is zero ambiguity regarding how a candidate can communicate with us.

3. On every Web page, include a rotating banner featuring photos of smiling employees. What does a proud parent do when you meet them? They show you pictures of their kids. If you're proud of your employees, show 'em off. Hire a professional to take posed photos — it's worth the couple hundred bucks — plus grab your digital camera

to snap casual photos of employees at company events. Not only will the photos make your company appear more personable to candidates, current team members will be happy to be featured on your website.

4. <u>Be clear.</u> Eliminate jargon and industry-specific acronyms that could confuse a potential candidate. Ask friends who know little about your organization to identify terms, phrases, and concepts that aren't 100% clear.

5. <u>Don't be shy about selling site visitors on why they should work for your company.</u> We created a page titled Reasons You Should Work For Jameson Publishing. It afforded us the chance to talk about our world-class employees, friendly work environment, company stability, superior compensation, premium benefits, professional growth, and comprehensive training programs. Some of our sales reps earn more than $100,000 a year. Why should we keep that a secret?

6. <u>Spend a little money to ensure that your site is professional.</u> If you know how to turn on a computer, you can launch a website. But just because you *can* doesn't mean you *should*. Don't cheap out and save a few hundred bucks by anointing yourself company webmaster. Find a competent partner to help you launch a professional-looking site. Choose a Web platform that gives you the ability to change the site as necessary so you don't have to outsource updates to a third party.

7. <u>Keep your website up to date.</u> In my company, an employee reviews specific pages on the site each month to ensure that the data is accurate. The area I've seen most neglected on company websites is the list of current job openings: Open jobs aren't listed; filled jobs are still being promoted.

8. <u>Proofread your site.</u> If a co-worker doesn't have this skill, find a low-cost, highly skilled proofreader online. Nothing screams second-rate company more loudly than "Qulaity Is Are #1 Goal!"

The goal of these recommendations is to ensure that visitors to your site not only are aware you have job openings but believe you are a desirable employer. Within 60 seconds of landing on your site, every visitor should feel genuinely excited about becoming part of your team.

Social Media

I won't say much about social media, but that's not because I question its effectiveness for your organization. Social media recruiting is evolving so quickly, anything I recommend would probably be passé by the time you read this. Research what social media tactics are working for organizations similar to yours, test what might fit your organization, then engage in only the most effective activities.

Newspaper Ads

If I'd assembled this list of best recruiting activities in the early 2000s, newspaper ads might have been #1. If you wrote a good ad for the Sunday paper, you could count on being inundated with résumés all week long. But newspaper ads have generated next to nothing for many companies, including mine, during the past two years. We still run an occasional classified ad just to make sure we don't miss out on a passive candidate (one not actively engaged in seeking a new job) who might be flipping through the paper.

Here are best practices we've learned about newspaper advertising:

- Pulse your classified ads. Running them several weeks in a row produces diminishing returns and, even more damaging, creates the impression of high turnover at your company.
- Entice readers with partial information about the position, but steer them to your website for a more complete description of the job and your company. You can't communicate your culture in a 5", 1-column ad.
- "You copy" is more engaging than "us copy." Example of "you copy": "If you're interested in working with a stable, local employer and a team of professionals, our sales position may be what you're looking for. As a sales representative, you will establish relationships with CEOs, vice presidents, and other executives to sell advertising for our magazines and websites. Your hard work will lead to personal and professional growth."

Employment Websites

List your open positions on employment websites, which many candidates browse for jobs, but brace for disappointment. You'll be burdened with the job of sorting through junk résumés from candidates who don't meet your minimum job requirements or who live in Booger Hole, West Virginia when your opening is in San Diego. Base your employment website strategy on my earlier advice about testing which social media sites work for you and writing "you copy" to steer job seekers to your company website.

Now it's time to build your list of most-effective recruiting activities. Use my list and examples as guidance, but don't misinterpret my company's preferences as the *Recruiting Bible* for your organization. Recruiting encompasses many unique market-specific, geography-specific, and job-specific challenges, so there isn't one action plan for every organization to follow. Your list, based on your experience, will serve as your navigator to recruiting success.

CHAPTER 10

Proven Pre-Employment Process

Get the Outcome. Don't Just "Run the Drill."

The actionable information and pre-employment questions on the remaining pages of this book are time-tested, proven best practices that will lead to more successful hiring at any company.

But they can also be dangerous.

Inexperienced hiring managers will use the questions like a person with a broken ankle uses crutches — leaning on them too hard. They will blindly follow each step without focusing on the outcomes and end goals for the process. They will "run the drill," asking the first question, then the second question, then the third. They will continue asking questions until time's up or they get to the end of the list. Every hiring manager in your organization needs to understand the *why* behind every question in order to align initial questions and follow-ups with interview outcomes. Don't jump to the questions at the end of this book just yet. Keep reading.

Hiring managers should develop an interviewing style that feels comfortable to them. This includes determining each interview's business and emotional outcomes, the wording and sequence of questions, and the general tone of the interview. Here's the message I've delivered to newer hiring managers: "This is your interview. You are responsible for determining if the candidate has the skills, personality, character, and mapping to work for our company. You are responsible for determining the outcomes of each interview and obtaining information that will help you make the best hiring decision. Don't focus on the process."

Questions do not need to be asked exactly as stated in Part IV of this book. Put them into your own words so you don't sound phony. The hiring manager's style and fundamental questions should be consistent; asking similar questions of each candidate provides a barometer to compare them with current employees and with other candidates for the same position.

The hiring manager should integrate managing expectations, establishing responsibilities, and your company's principles throughout the interview process (i.e., Set Them Up For Future Reference). Throughout every interview, let candidates know exactly what they are signing up for and what remaining employed with your company will require. Use blunt facts and candor. You are not selling the candidates on the job; you are giving and getting data.

Here are excerpts from a letter to sales candidates that we integrated into the Final Aversions Interview of our pre-employment process. After reading this, let me know if we've clearly painted a picture of what the candidate is signing up for.

- "During your interview process, we intended to clearly convey the basic values of our company and what the sales job entails. During the interview process, we have outlined the traits that it takes to be successful in this sales job. You have advanced this far in our interview process because we believe you have the ability to do the job. However, it will likely be your decision as to whether you will accept the job. Before you make that decision, please ask yourself this question: 'Am I willing to make the commitment to transform a sales territory into a growing "franchise"?' But before you answer that question, we'd like to give you a clearer picture of what your sales career with us may be like. This document will give you an indication of what you may encounter and achieve in this job."

- "Transforming your sales territory with us into a sustainable, stable 'franchise' takes time. In fact, we believe it will take you years to fully potentialize this opportunity. All the while, you'll be encouraged to develop your skills around our sales process, sales call quality, account management, and sales-related travel. Your leadership and marketing abilities will also be tested and improved."

- "This skill-building journey with us, that leads toward independence and stability, should be enriching. As with any challenging process, however, there are times when salespeople become frustrated with themselves, the company, or their colleagues."

- "These occasions will test your emotional control and your commitment to becoming successful. Our successful salespeople view these instances as motivational opportunities that help them grow and, ultimately, reach their full potential. The company is going to be imperfect. Part of your job is, at times, to help fix the things that would improve us."

- "Our company and you have the same shared goal — for you to build a personally and professionally rewarding sales career. We will work with you at monthly goal-setting meetings to evaluate and test the health of your sales funnel and pace of account movement. Periodically, we will audit your 'franchise' to help you avoid a potential sales slump in the future. If your 'franchise' is healthy, then these goal-setting meetings and periodic audits will be an opportunity to understand how you work most effectively. And your supervisor can learn how to best support your activities."

- "How quickly and how well you achieve the result of transforming your territory into a 'franchise' will depend largely on three components:
  ○ Initiative — You will decide how fast you get results at this job. The more initiative you take, the faster you will advance. We know the difficulties you will encounter, and we already know many of the solutions or how to get you to the solutions. Your responsibility is to learn where to go to get the information you need that will get you to the solution you are seeking.
  ○ Discipline — The more discipline you apply, the less bureaucracy and management labor we will be required to spend on you. This lowers our overhead (business expenses); the lower the overhead, the stronger the business. You will largely determine how much management you need. Without initiative and discipline, our relationship will prove to be a frustrating mismatch and will end due to this mismatch.
  ○ Best Practices — Your results will depend on your willingness to learn and perform the best practices we've developed over time. These best practices are simply crutches to build successful habits and support any performance weaknesses you may have. You'll need initiative and discipline to apply these best practices and incorporate your own unique abilities and talents. How you personalize these best practices

with your own sales style will go a long way to determining how you develop and advance your career."

- "If you ever feel we are not adhering to the concepts outlined here with you or anyone else, we would truly appreciate you making us aware of it. If you don't understand the reason behind an action or policy, or you don't believe appropriate changes are being made — and your supervisor is not able to adequately make changes that align with our principles or help you to understand why we are doing what we do — please let me know. We would like you to continue to go upline (to the president or a Steering Committee member, if necessary) until you reach an answer that is reasonable to you. We are striving to make this a fair and safe work environment where high character, self-governing, independent-thinking people thrive — both at work and in life."

That's a mouthful, eh? We implemented that language because our sales job is unlike most other sales jobs, and our company is unlike most other organizations. We thought it would be a disservice to candidates, their families, our team, and our company if we didn't spell out the challenge. Please note there's a lot of discussion around these topics to provide context for the challenge; we don't just print the letter and hand it to candidates at their first interview.

Employee Hiring Process

We develop a detailed *Employee Hiring Process* planning document for every open position in our company. There are four reasons we do this:

1. To establish a structure for hiring employees. You want to develop your pre-employment plan before you start interviewing candidates.

2. To ensure that important details have been thought through prior to the new position being approved by senior management.

3. To ensure that all required documentation and information is available prior to advertising or recruiting for a position.

4. To ensure that all employees involved in the hiring process are aware of the established targets for this position.

Prior to presenting senior management a motion to hire a new employee, the requesting hiring manager completes the Employee Hiring Process planning document and emails it to the HR director, all employees mentioned in the document (who will participate in interviews), and the company president. The hiring manager is responsible for contacting recipients who do not respond by the specified deadline or who have questions or request more information about the document.

The completed Employee Hiring Process document consists of nine sections:

1. Title and Management
   a. Title of position.
   b. Name of hiring manager.
   c. Who will conduct the employee's annual review?
   d. Who will notice when the employee doesn't have enough work or is wasting time?
   e. Who will assign the employee additional tasks?
   f. Who will notice when the employee makes mistakes and performs less than best practice?

2. Job Description

3. Pay Structure
   a. List bonuses, incentives, and commissions that will be in addition to base pay.

4. Testing requirements
   a. Names of specific tests and target scores. Scores below the target are identified as an aversion.

5. Interview Process, including the names of specific employee(s) who will conduct that step
   a. Phone Screen: Fundamental questions about the job to determine if a first interview is appropriate.
   b. 1st Meeting: Pre-employment testing and first interview.
   c. 2nd Meeting: Second interview; candidate completes background check authorization documents.
   d. 3rd Meeting: Spend time at our office shadowing employees (if necessary), plus a third interview.
   e. Hiring manager conducts reference checks.
   f. 4th Meeting: Dinner Interview.
   g. Validation/final approval: Hiring manager discusses the candidate with the company president.
   h. 5th Meeting: Final Aversions Interview.

      i.   Job Offer (via phone).
         Note: Conduct at least one additional interview for management or executive candidates.

6. Training program
    a. A summary of the training process for the position.

7. Required targets/skills. Candidates must, at a minimum, have these qualifications to enter the hiring process.

8. Preferred targets/skills. We prefer candidates have these qualifications, but they are not requirements to enter the hiring process.

9. Metrics and/or reports to measure performance.

We don't relax after the candidate accepts our job offer. We instruct candidates to call the hiring manager between the job offer and their first day to share how their quit notice went. Then we instruct candidates to call the hiring manager once a week with any questions or thoughts or just to touch base. This is especially important if the first day will be two weeks or more after your job offer. You want the candidate, who is still a free agent, to remain tethered to the hiring manager rather than continue interviewing with other companies.

The hiring manager should meet with any employee who will train the new hire. Using specifics from the candidate's interview, they discuss the plan to overcome the candidate's aversions, how the hiring manager Set Them Up For Future Reference, and the candidate's strengths. The goal is that the trainer and hiring manager have the same understanding of the situation and agree on the action plan to successfully manage the new hire. They should regularly discuss the new hire's progress. The hiring manager needs to have a full understanding of how the new hire is progressing. Is the employee advancing on the aversions identified during the interview process? Have any new issues emerged? When appropriate, the hiring manager should be involved in the trainer's personnel-related discussions with the new hire.

CHAPTER 11

Uncovering, Exposing, & Overcoming Aversions

Uncovering and handling aversions is the heart — and undeniably the most difficult aspect — of pre-employment interviews. Aversions rarely jump out of the candidate's mouth and pop you in the nose. You have to dig for them and apply discernment if you uncover them. It's not even as easy as the number of aversions you uncover. I've worked with hiring managers who thought a candidate should automatically be eliminated if 10 or more aversions were uncovered during the interview process. But that's incorrect thinking. The ultimate question is: "Are the candidate's aversions manageable?"

Because there are no perfect candidates, you should uncover multiple aversions for every candidate. If you hold out for a seemingly perfect candidate, your company will suffer because you won't be able to hire at the pace necessary to grow your business. As I stated three sentences ago, you need to determine if the candidate's aversions are *manageable*. Will they prevent the candidate from succeeding at your company? Will the candidate be able to improve to an acceptable level of performance within a reasonable time with a reasonable amount of management?

The hiring manager is responsible for uncovering important aversions during interviews and developing the right questions to gain data to confirm or eliminate each aversion. Uncovering and addressing important aversions can protect your company from making bad hires. This technique will also enable you to make *good* hires *better* by immediately starting them on the path to overcoming their aversions and improving their weaknesses by Setting Them Up For Future Reference.

Uncovering Aversions

Tailor your interview questions to learn more about potential aversions you have about the candidate. We've stated this before, but it's worth repeating: Do not base a conclusion about an aversion on just one or two data points. Instead of allowing your assumptions to fill in the blanks, ask probing questions to get a full understanding of the situation and reasons for the candidate's behavior. Get specifics! Only then will you have the right to determine if the aversion is real.

Hiring managers often jump to discuss aversions without validating whether the aversions are real. Don't race to verbalize a potential aversion. Be empathetic and encourage candidates to speak their mind before revealing an aversion to them.

Another common mistake of hiring managers is being too direct with questions. Most candidates will know how to spin their answers if they know what you're digging for. They will show you the face you want to see, not exposing the whole truth about themselves. Casual, conversational, benign questions are non-threatening and their intent is more difficult to detect. Friendly, innocuous comments allow candidates to feel comfortable to continue without filtering their answers. This will allow you to learn what's in them.

Example of a non-threatening conversation that uncovers an aversion: To determine how much trouble a candidate has with supervision, you ask him to explain career progression from one job to the next across his résumé. You casually ask open-ended questions about anything relevant along the way. The candidate may feel you're on his side and in agreement as he explains why each successive company's managers were "horrible" because they wanted him to complete reports on time and accurately.

Once you expose your potential aversion to the candidate, there is no turning back. So be sure to exhaust your questions without revealing your aversion.

Exposing Aversions

Historical evidence is the strongest proof for confirming or eliminating candidates' aversions. How they behaved over time is a fairly accurate forecast of their future behavior. Exposing the aversion is a last step. Take that step only after you have exhausted every other option of gathering historical evidence.

Once you are absolutely convinced of an aversion's validity and have evidence the candidate can't overcome it by revealing additional historical data, expose the aversion. Set the stage by explaining why a frank discussion of the aversion is in the best interests of both the candidate and your company. This will help put the candidate at ease while adding enormous significance to the conversation's outcome. It will also expose how issues needing improvement could affect the candidate's future at your company.

- Example: "This job is a lot about listening. And when you talk, you can't listen. When you're talking long, you can't pay attention. Here are a few examples of you talking long. (Detail examples.) In this job, you need to be a good listener. As we move forward, we need to find out if you can be a good listener, because it's vital to you being successful in this job."

- Example: "I've seen a lot of reasons why you would like our job and why we would like you. (Briefly list the reasons.) But one thing I've picked up through the interview that concerns me is (insert aversion). I'm concerned that will cause you to not like this job very much."

Another time to expose aversions is when you have more or less decided you are eliminating the candidate. Share key aversions so these candidates know why you're eliminating them. Example: "I haven't decided if this is a fit, but here's what I'm thinking right now. (List key aversions.)" You don't have to share every aversion with the candidate, especially the aversions that will unnecessarily create hard feelings (e.g., bad breath, arrogance, lack of personality). That conversation will be a train wreck, no matter how carefully you choose your words.

I've exposed aversions while not offending the candidate by turning a trait that wouldn't be a fit at our company into a compliment. For candidates who are pushy, too direct, controlling, and don't get along with co-workers, I say something like, "I haven't decided if this is a fit. But here's what I'm thinking right now. Our environment is very structured, and you'll get feedback from lots of different people. I think someone like you would probably find it stifling. Have you ever considered owning your own company or starting your own company? There are a lot of successful entrepreneurs with your personality traits." Almost 100% of the candidates agree that could be the case, and we spend a few minutes talking about their interest in self-employment and my experience as a small-business owner. Business and emotional outcomes achieved. Train wreck avoided.

For candidates you don't plan to eliminate, find a push/pull balance when exposing aversions. You want to make sure that you've indicated you may want to hire them. You want to emphasize your company liking them, but continue to let them know that you're still determining if they're a match for the job. Don't give an overly positive or overly negative picture of the situation. Balance the pain of the job — not sugar-coating it — with some of the great things about it. Example with a sales candidate: "You're going to have to get up early every morning and pound the phones every day, but you'll have the opportunity to make more than $100,000."

Don't wait until the Final Aversions Interview or late in your interview process to address core aversions. It's better to have candidates know your aversions so they can overcome them or move on to another company after you have exhausted every other option. We have a saying around our office that applies to interviews (and healthy co-worker communication in general): "Let them know when you know, always."

If you eliminate candidates without exposing aversions, you will not achieve your intended emotional outcome. Candidates will perceive that you eliminated them because you didn't like them. They will assume the worst: that their elimination was not due to anything they did, but was the fault of the interviewer and the fault of your company. When asked why they didn't get the job, they will say, "I don't know. They didn't like me. I know I could do that job. They're crazy." Even worse, eliminated candidates who are members of a protected class could sue your company for illegal discrimination.

Compare those emotions with this scenario in which the hiring manager shares the aversions with the candidate: "There are many reasons I think you can do this job. But my biggest aversion is that you have been self-employed for the past five years and will not adapt to the structured environment of our inside sales job. I think you'd be better suited for an outside sales job that has more flexibility."

Disclosure gives the candidate a chance to overcome your aversions. Also, if you call to inform them that they've been eliminated from your hiring process, they will know why they were eliminated. When asked why they didn't get the job, they can say they're better suited for outside sales.

The biggest risk you run by exposing aversions to candidates is offending them with your explanation. The risks you run by not exposing aversions is harming your company's reputation as a fair employer in your community and inciting a candidate to seek litigation.

It's your call.

Overcoming Aversions

A key purpose of uncovering and exposing aversions is to give the candidate a chance to overcome them. You have confirmed the aversion exists and want to find out if the candidate can manage it. It's the candidate's last chance for redemption. If they can't overcome important aversions, they understand why you did not extend a job offer. Overcoming the aversions gives you both a head start on areas the candidate needs to improve in order to succeed at your company. Consider this the first phase of managing the new employee.

The hiring manager needs to understand what the core aversions are and how they will harm the candidate's work performance, then determine if the candidate can overcome them. Example: A candidate's larger-than-normal ego is not the true aversion. The true aversion is how that ego manifests itself in the workplace. Can the candidate manage that behavior?

There are two ways to overcome aversions. The best method is to obtain factual evidence in the candidate's history that validates or invalidates your aversion. That's essentially the focus of this book, especially the section on *Behavior-Focused Interviewing.* But sometimes you need to utilize an alternative technique to achieve your outcome.

That alternative is a one-for-one test that requires candidates to do exactly what you want them to incline to do as employees. My company asks every candidate moving to a second interview to write a 700–900 word essay on a lesson learned from life experiences. At the close of the first interview, we hand the candidate directions that include topic, word count, deadline, and where to email the essay. We are testing reading comprehension, ability to follow multiple directions and meet a deadline, thought process for selecting an appropriate topic, and communication skills.

Common one-for-one tests include:

- For sales candidates: Role-play a sales call. Set the scenario, allow time for candidates to prepare for the call, have them talk with a co-worker posing as a prospect, then watch how they conduct themselves during the call. Afterward, ask them to evaluate their performance.
- For marketing candidates: Give them 20 minutes to write you a persuasive letter/email.
- For manager candidates: Test business acumen, critical thinking, and communication skills by asking them to write a brief business plan and present it to you at the next interview.

Want detailed examples of one-for-one tests? Here you go:

- A sales candidate claimed to have no problem accepting criticism, but one of our aversions of him was no history of receiving regular feedback from a supervisor. About a half-hour into his second interview, the hiring manager said, "You say you're OK with criticism. Can I give you some?" The candidate replied, "Sure." The hiring manager stated, directly yet unemotionally, that almost all of the candidate's answers during the interview had been lengthy and vague. If he's unable to communicate better with customers, he won't be a successful rep for us. So for the rest of the interview, we'd like him to answer more succinctly and with as many specifics as he can provide. A healthy reaction from the candidate would have been "No problem. Thanks for the feedback." and improvement for the rest of our conversation. Instead, the candidate became red-faced with embarrassment, slumped in his chair, and clammed up for the rest of the interview. We even coached him that his two-sentence responses weren't what we were looking for either. But the pressure was too much for him, and the rest of the interview proved to us that he couldn't accept constructive criticism.

- I was interviewing a sales candidate who gave extremely long-winded answers to the first three questions I asked. He even interrupted himself once to ask, "Uh, what was the question you asked me?" For the fourth question — which could have been answered in 30 seconds — I kept my eye on the clock to see how long it took him to answer. (Side note: The glass on the conference room table let me watch the reflection of the clock without making it obvious I was timing the answer. Pretty sneaky, huh?) After the candidate completed his seemingly 2,000-word reply, I asked how long he thought he'd taken to answer that question. He thought two or three minutes. I told him it was exactly 7 minutes, 45 seconds and admitted I was watching the clock. I detailed how he strayed from the topic we were discussing and what he could have cut out to give me the answer I needed. Wanting to test his ability to control his conversation (the aversion), I asked him to keep his answers for the rest of our interview under four minutes. If I wanted more information, I'd ask him to continue. He agreed. His next answer was succinct, so I complimented him for that. But his subsequent answers were all over 5 minutes (some nearly 10 minutes), so we eliminated him from the process. This one-for-one test proved that he was unable to control his verbal communication.

- For writer candidates, our company learned the hard way that we needed a one-for-one test to gauge the important skills of interviewing for a story, organizing the data gathered, and writing the article. We'd hired a few editor candidates who presented well and boasted relevant experience, but failed to produce quality articles for us after we hired them. So we implemented a writer test in which one of our senior editors plays the subject of a story for one of our magazines and the candidate conducts the interview, organizes the data, and writes a brief story. This all-day process has saved us time, labor, and thousands of dollars by providing data that caused us to eliminate several unqualified candidates from our hiring process. It gave us confidence that candidates who passed the test could do the job and made them more eager to accept our job offer.

Discuss results of one-for-one tests with candidates. Don't eliminate candidates just because they failed a single one-for-one test (unless it's a cataclysmic failure). Show them where they fell short, give them another chance, and see if they make appropriate adjustments and improvement. Be careful not to overvalue a successful one-for-one test. Performing the one-for-one test doesn't mean candidates can (or will want to) do that for the rest of their life.

When candidates cannot overcome the aversion and are too great a risk to hire, we sometimes send them away to get a similar job with another local company and ask them to call us in a year to see how they like that line of work. We usually do this with recent college graduates or candidates who are changing careers. It's the ultimate one-for-one test: Try it for 12 months, then let's look at the results.

A one-for-one test should not be confused with simply exposing candidates to the circumstance they will have trouble with (the aversion). Examples of activities that are <u>not</u> one-for-one tests: sales candidates spending time with your sales department, observing sales calls and a sales meeting; manager candidates observing manager/employee meetings; and operations candidates talking with employees about the stresses they'll face on the job.

One More Thing About Aversions …

In my company's history, hiring managers have often been too harsh when determining if candidates can overcome their aversions. We eliminated good candidates from our process because we did not apply critical thinking and appropriate discernment. Here are two good methods to test whether you are applying appropriate discernment or being unreasonably harsh:

1. Draft a mini-annual review to help the candidate to overcome the biggest aversions.

   - How much of your labor and effort does the plan require? If it's an unacceptable amount long term, you probably should not offer that candidate a job.
   - Is the plan executable? If there is a very slim chance of successfully executing this plan, you probably should not offer this candidate a job. If your company is skilled and generally successful at helping people overcome the candidate's major aversions, you might want to make the offer.
   - Understand that any new hire will require your management labor. Some new hires will be difficult to get to standard but will be well worth the effort. Your goal should not be to hire only candidates who are easy to manage from the outset of their career with your company.

2. Apply the same discernment and skepticism you have for the candidate to current co-workers of yours who are now above-standard but weren't when they came on board. Would they have been eliminated or hired based on your rationale? Some of my company's all-time best hires had several major areas to improve when we hired them. But we saw their potential, managed them closely, and gave them more than one chance to succeed. Here are a few examples:

   - Tracy applied for a sales job. Her only professional experience was as a chemist, but Tracy showed us that she had the character, mapping, and personality to work in sales. She's been a successful sales manager for over eight years, managing millions of dollars in revenue and earning a spot on our company's annual sales-goal trip.
   - All John's sales experience was in outside sales or retail sales, so he had very little of the phone experience our inside sales position involved. After on-the-job training, he helped generate millions of dollars in sales for our company and advanced to become our VP of publishing.
   - Jon was in his 20s when we interviewed him. He lacked serious attention to work, which appeared to be a poor work ethic. With strong management, he functioned up. Now vice president of sales and marketing, he successfully steers the activities of many sales managers and sales reps.

As I stated before, don't look for angels. Many of my company's best employees have committed egregious mistakes with past employers. Some were even fired. Probe to determine if candidates have learned from their mistakes and changed their behavior accordingly. Are they willing to accept criticism and work earnestly to correct their problems?

CHAPTER 12

General Interview Best Practices Policies & Procedures

The following pages include actions you should take during all phases of your pre-employment interview process. I'd have integrated these best practices into the other chapters in this book if I were a more talented writer. But I'm not. So here you go.

1. **Conducting your interview without proper preparation is unacceptable.** If you have not thoroughly prepared for the interview by the time the candidate arrives at your office, you should greet the candidate and say, "I need some time to prepare for our interview. Please give me a few minutes." Prepare at your desk before you begin the interview. Conducting an interview without proper preparation is a choice, and it is a choice to fail. If this is a recurring behavior, know that this is not acceptable, and take corrective action. Or call me and I'll yell at you until you cry.

   Prepare for your interview by thoroughly reviewing all the information, looking for potential aversions and areas about which you need to gather more information. Then define the business and emotional outcomes for your interview. Next, detail your action plan to achieve those outcomes. Take time before the interview to put the questions in your own words. But make sure they're phrased in a way that will achieve the business and emotional outcomes you desire.

Develop a contingency plan. Consider what answers the candidate might give to your initial questions and develop follow-up questions that focus on helping you achieve your business and emotional outcomes. What will you do if your original questions do not achieve your intended outcomes? What questions will you ask then?

2. **To avoid potential legal conflicts, avoid these topics during the interview.** Do not initiate conversations on:
   1. Age (for candidates 40 and over)
   2. Marital status
   3. Sexual orientation
   4. Pregnancy/children
   5. Religion
   6. Citizenship/race/national origin
   7. Medical conditions
   8. Potential disabilities or handicaps, including addictions

   Don't panic if the candidate brings up one of these topics during your interview. It doesn't mean you and your company are going to be sued. Just move away from that subject and make sure all your questions or comments are aligned with appropriate outcomes.

   Realize that laws change. Establish a relationship with a world-class labor attorney you can consult with as appropriate. The money you pay that attorney up front will be considerably less than the money (and time) you'll spend defending yourself if your hiring managers and your interview process are out of legal compliance.

3. **Do not make or imply promises to the candidate.** This could cause a legal liability for your company, especially with reference to pay. Example: A sales candidate says, early in the process, "I'm looking to start at $50,000 base pay." The interviewer should not say, "That shouldn't be a problem." The interviewer *should* say, "That's not out of the question. If we get close to a job offer, we will talk more specifically about pay and what salary would be appropriate for someone with your skill set."

   Don't give the candidate the upper range of what you would pay for the job.

Example: An accounting candidate who currently makes $30,000 a year would like to start a new job at $35,000. When the candidate asks how much your company pays new-hire accountants, the hiring manager should not say, "Some of our accountants started at $40,000." When offered the job at $35,000, this candidate could be offended to be $5,000 below that range even though the offer is the amount the candidate originally wanted.

Handing a note with pay information to a candidate can be considered a job offer. If you do not later extend a job offer, that candidate could sue you for the amount indicated on the note.

Don't incorrectly Set Them Up For Future Reference and mismanage their expectations, such as the candidate's anticipated career path. Example: A sales candidate says, "I'd like to be a sales manager in two years." The hiring manager should not say, "If you work hard, hit your sales goals, and act like a leader, you'll be a sales manager." The hiring manager should say, "We look for good sales managers all the time. If you succeed as a sales rep, we can talk in more detail about a career path that might include a manager role."

4. **Gather information that will answer your fundamental interview questions and uncover important aversions until you determine you will eliminate the candidate.** As soon as data leads you to conclude that you will eliminate the candidate, you should fast track that candidate. *Fast Tracking* is the act of wrapping up the interview as quickly as possible without causing a negative emotional outcome. There is little benefit to your company to have you continue a lengthy discussion with a candidate you know will be eliminated. You should have better things to do. You're better off taking a nap for an hour rather than wasting a second hour talking with a candidate you won't hire. With the nap, at least you'll be rested afterwards.

5. **Take thorough notes so you base your hiring decision on details of the candidate's answers.** Use silence to give yourself time to take better notes. There is no rush. You control the pace of the interview.

Make all your notes in ink. Pencil fades over time and, because it can be erased, does not ensure accurate record-keeping. Using a different color ink at each interview makes it easier to distinguish at which stage of the interview process you uncovered specific information.

6. **Don't conduct one-on-one interviews after hours.** Doing so can create an unnecessary risk that your company doesn't need to take on, especially if one of the parties is male and one is female. The candidate — whom you don't know at all — could make a harassment claim against your interviewer, which would be one's words against the other's. It's a legal battle guaranteed to cost you time and money. If a candidate can meet you only after hours, make sure two of your employees are in the room or in your building for the interview.

7. **Reference checks and background checks should be conducted on all candidates prior to a job offer.** I recommend the reference check be conducted by the hiring manager, not delegated to someone in HR. The hiring manager is best qualified to discuss specifics of the job and have a supervisor-to-supervisor discussion about the candidate's strengths and weaknesses.

   Reference check questions should be aversion-based. Don't ask only questions that are broad in scope (e.g., *Can you tell me about John Smith?*). Ask questions about aversions you have uncovered (e.g., *Can you give me examples of John reacting to criticism? Any examples of him reacting poorly to criticism?*).

   You are legally permitted to call past employers even if the candidate hasn't listed them. Here's an example of when that tactic worked for my company: A candidate provided us with several business references, each of whom gave positive feedback. A co-worker of mine was an acquaintance of the candidate's former boss (who wasn't listed as a reference) and called to get his perspective. The former boss said the candidate left his company because he was caught stealing and that several co-workers thanked him for firing the man, whose arrogance regularly offended them. "I wouldn't hire him again if you gave me a million dollars," said the former boss. I'm sure glad we made that extra call.

8. **Push for the quickest pace that will be effective, but don't rush through any steps related to the interview process** — preparation, the interview itself, post-interview analysis, downloading information

to co-workers involved in the hiring process. Like anything else, doing this right might take more time but will be more effective.

9. **Do not add unnecessary lag time to your hiring process.** Our company calls it *Air in the System.* Qualified candidates are difficult to find. You do not want to lose a strong candidate because other potential employers are moving faster than you are. At the end of each interview, say that if you don't call within one or two business days, the candidate should call you. This not only reduces Air in the System, it tests the candidate's ability to follow your directions.

CHAPTER 13

The Dinner Interview

At the foundation of your pre-employment interview process, you need to learn about candidates as people, as opposed to just asking questions to get answers. You need to know what's *inside* candidates. The only way to do that is to spend time with them, and not just during in-office interviews. So I recommend including a Dinner Interview as part of your hiring process. Invite the candidate and spouse or significant other to dine at a nice restaurant with you and your spouse/significant other.

Yes, it's unusual to involve spouses in an interview process. But you want to get close to the candidate's spouse because people spend most of their time at their job and the second most time with their spouse. This new job will affect both the candidate and the candidate's spouse, so they should make this decision together. An opportunity to ask and answer questions gives the spouse the opportunity to be an active part of this decision and provides firsthand exposure to your company. Otherwise, the spouse's decision is based only on information filtered by the candidate, who generally doesn't share as much information as the spouse would like. The spouse can help the candidate decide about taking the job because the spouse often knows better than the candidate if the candidate can overcome the aversions you have. The spouse can gauge if the candidate will overcome your aversions and be successful in your environment. Plus, for future management purposes, you can find out if the spouse will be a drain on the candidate and not support the job or will act as a promoter of your company.

Another reason I like the Dinner Interview is because it helps you achieve your emotional outcomes. It's conducted late in your interview process, after the candidate has spent several pressure-packed hours answering your questions and has *earned* this perk. Being wined and dined by your company makes any candidate feel special. Most candidates I've interviewed over dinner had never been treated to a meal during a pre-employment process, so they felt like a big deal when we asked them to dinner.

You might be skeptical that a meal interview with the candidate's spouse is necessary. So let me share a story about when I fouled up this step and almost cost my company dearly. We had been searching for months for a candidate to fill our open customer service manager position, and Connie's skills seemed a near-perfect fit for the job. She was professional, but not overly personable, so she didn't open up much about any topics outside of the office. The Dinner Interview with her husband, when we'd have to talk about more than work history, could have been an excellent opportunity to get to know Connie as a person. But Connie's husband was out of town on a construction job, so we either had to wait to have dinner with both of them or take Connie to lunch by herself. In my haste to fill the position, I told Connie we'd do lunch without her husband. The lunch was pleasant, but didn't provide key information we needed about Connie as a person. We didn't fully understand to what degree her life outside of work would affect her job. When I called to offer Connie the job, she said she'd accept only if we offered her flextime so she could leave early to take her daughter to skating practice whenever necessary. I never saw that coming. I couldn't change our company's work hours to accommodate Connie, especially because so many co-workers and customers count on our customer service managers to be there when needed. She declined the job offer, and we went back to the drawing board.

If Connie hadn't been forthright with me and had requested flextime after accepting the position, we'd have been in quite a quandary — all because I didn't get the information I needed before making the job offer. I really dodged a bullet there. This story actually has a happy ending. Weeks later, we interviewed and eventually hired Lynn as our customer service manager. She *and her husband* were excellent company at the Dinner Interview, and she's been a tremendous asset to our team for over a decade.

Prior to the Dinner Interview, prepare your significant other regarding the candidate's aversions and what you want to discuss at the dinner. (If the hiring manager doesn't have a significant other, it's appropriate to invite an employee from the group the candidate would work with. Even if the candidate does not have a spouse/significant other, conduct a meal interview in order to reap the benefits outlined later in this chapter.)

Your preparation for the Dinner Interview should:

- Outline who is going to talk, how much, and what to talk about when. I'd sometimes make a cheat sheet of key questions we wanted to ask or points we wanted to make during the dinner. I rarely had to consult it, but when I'd use the restroom during the meal, I glanced at it to make sure we didn't miss anything. (Sorry for being so uptight. Remember, one candidate did yell at me for being anal.)

- Talk through important aversions. Include your significant other in what you're trying to accomplish. Encourage your partner to do anything unique that will help achieve your outcomes. My wife always did an excellent job asking how the spouse would handle the candidate's work and travel schedule. Her questions were sincere, because she could talk about how my schedule impacted our family.

- Be sure your partner understands what topics to steer clear of to help your company avoid potential legal conflicts. Don't assume your partner knows what to avoid. I can't tell you how many executives I've met who think it's A-OK to ask a woman her family plans in an interview setting.

- Be sure you have a functioning credit card or cash to cover the dinner. Imagine how you and your company would look if the candidate had to pick up the bill! You'd *have to* make a job offer just to recover from your screw-up.

The Dinner Interview allows my company to:

1. **Validate aversions; gather more information on aversions**. It's not normal to uncover additional new aversions at the dinner. (But keep looking for them!) You *will* gather more data on aversions already uncovered. The candidate's aversions determine how light or intense the conversation will be. Certain aversions —commitment to the area, whether the candidate will truly enjoy the demands of the job — may warrant more intense discussion. Insight from the candidate's spouse may enable you to confirm or eliminate an aversion. For example, we had an aversion that a sales candidate might leave us when the job got hard and return to his old job. His spouse said at dinner that she was

more than OK with him going back to his old job and told him to maintain his relationships there just in case. That didn't mean we automatically eliminated him from the process, but it led to intense conversation about this important aversion. The spouse can also provide further insight into aversions you've identified. By asking if they've talked about the aversion, you'll learn if the candidate told the truth about it and the spouse's reaction to it.

2. **Uncover new aversions.** Having dinner with a candidate works to your advantage only if you believe you have uncovered all aversions. You may be surprised at the valuable new information you can gain from what appears to be irrelevant conversation. Deeper truths than what you typically get in an interview will emerge over the entree. Example: The couple talks about how they like to travel frequently, but are disappointed by accommodations at every hotel. They also make unwarranted complaints about the service at the restaurant. Another example: A candidate I'd interviewed repeatedly teased his wife during dinner. He told stories she didn't want him to tell and talked himself up while poking fun at her. Guess what happened after we hired him? He acted the same way with his co-workers, and we terminated him before our good employees quit.

3. **Test the level of support from the spouse.** A spouse who isn't on board with the job requirements makes it tough for a candidate — especially in the first few months. Doing a good job is tough enough, and a disgruntled spouse only intensifies the struggle. Gauge whether the spouse will support your company when times are tough or encourage the candidate to quit. Is the candidate's spouse enthused or neutral about your company? Does the spouse feel the candidate can do the job? Will the spouse enjoy the job? Why? The spouse should be as excited about the new job as the candidate. A good example is Ed, a candidate for operations manager, and his wife Melissa. Ed managed a retail store and Melissa was an emergency room nurse. Both jobs required long and irregular hours and dealing with people in unusual circumstances. Ed, who had worked in retail for 20 years, had told us that his main motivation when applying for our job was wanting a bigger challenge and regular hours. How would his wife feel about him switching his career path? She spoke passionately about how the job would be an upgrade for Ed and their entire family. She took time to ask friends and co-workers what they had heard about our company's reputation and told us the feedback was all positive. So we knew that

when Ed's job got tough, Melissa would support him and encourage him to stay, not press him to return to retail.

4. **Provide information to help the spouse support the employee; demonstrate your reasonableness and resources to solve work problems.** These three examples should shed more light on this hard-to-visualize concept:

Example A: My company has a bottom-up approach to identifying and solving problems. So we inform the employee and the employee's spouse that anyone who identifies a problem in the company can go as far upline as necessary to resolve it. Our president wants to hear about problems that aren't being resolved. So the spouse knows that an employee who complains about a problem has the ability to resolve it.

Example B: We share details about the demands of our inside sales job (required daily phone time, calls critiqued by their manager, travel demands, sales goals, etc.). So the spouse knows what the employee signed up for and knows, if the employee complains about the job, that we haven't made any new demands.

Example C: We specify the difficulties of the sales cycles of our inside sales job, especially early on. New reps sell lower-priced products during training, then typically hit a post-training slump before making sales on bigger-ticket items. Our reps produce a smaller volume of sales (with larger dollar amounts per sale) than most traditional jobs. *No* is the typical answer to: "Did you sell anything today?" The father of a young sales rep we'd recently hired warned his son that he'd be fired if he didn't make a sale each week. That's how Dad thought all sales worked. Our new rep fought through the stress those comments caused, but I wish we'd had the opportunity to talk with his father about the rigors of our job.

5. **Sell the spouse on the job.** Be realistic about the struggles the candidate will face, but emphasize that the rewards for the hard work are great. When you provide info that could push the candidate and spouse away, you have to provide info that will pull them in slightly stronger. Example: "You'll need to sell a higher-priced product than you're selling now. That will be a challenge, but you'll also have an opportunity to make more money than you're currently making." Or "Our sales job won't require you to run the wheels off your car or put in a lot of night

or weekend hours. You'll be home for dinner on a regular basis." Reinforce that your job meets the candidate's primary needs.

6. **Sell the spouse on the company.** The Dinner Interview is intended to heighten the spouse's excitement about the candidate joining your company. Emphasize that joining and eventually retiring from your company is worth the risk of leaving their current employer. Show that working for you is an upgrade by talking about your company's financial stability, higher pay, appropriate policies, and first-rate benefits. Also discuss how typical overtime and reasonable travel schedules allow employees to balance work and family time. Mention the friendly work atmosphere, tenure of current employees, your company's participation in growing markets, and future growth plans. The opportunity to ask questions and meet the candidate's future boss makes the spouse more comfortable with your company.

- Answer all their questions about the job.
- Give the spouse the opportunity to ask how a non-company representative (hiring manager's spouse) feels about the job and the company.
- Meeting the people who make your company what it is lets the candidate's spouse see the company's human side. The Dinner Interview establishes a personal connection between your company, the candidate, and the candidate's spouse.

7. **See how the candidate behaves in a more casual setting.** This can provide insight into how the candidate will behave with customers and co-workers in a social setting. Does the candidate dominate the conversation? Show good manners? Drink too much? Make a mess?

We encourage candidates to set the time and date of the Dinner Interview and to select a nice restaurant their spouse would like as a treat — not a five-star establishment, but a step above chains like Applebee's and T.G.I. Friday's. This positions your company a level above other employers that candidates have worked for or might be interviewing with. Clarifying that appropriate attire is "country club casual" — dress pants, dress shirt, and no necktie for men; skirt or dress slacks for women — helps create a comfortable mood.

To achieve the maximum value from the Dinner Interview, the candidate and their spouse need to be comfortable. Warming up is the key to getting them comfortable. Warm-up techniques include:

- Not jumping to your interview questions immediately. Get to know the couple personally.
- Prefacing the meal by asking, "Have you ever been to dinner with a prospective employer or do you know people who have?"
- Saying "We asked you to dinner, which is a little unusual. Most companies don't do this." Explain that you realize what a big decision a job change represents and that the purpose of this interview is to give the candidate and spouse a chance to learn about your company in a non-business setting and make sure all their questions are answered. Their feedback could guide the opening conversation.
- Before asking questions, talk about your work environment and your own experiences. Expose the struggles of the job by using yourself as an example or detail the experiences of others at your company: "My first year was a difficult adjustment. Here's how my wife and I handled it."

Conducting the Dinner Interview prior to the Final Aversions Interview lets you drill down and validate the candidate's aversions. If the Dinner Interview were the final step in your interview process, there would be no opportunity for one-on-one discussion of new aversions that arise at the restaurant. The day after the Dinner Interview, the hiring manager should meet with others who have interviewed the candidate to discuss what was said while breaking bread.

CHAPTER 14

The Final Aversions Interview

As outlined in *Uncovering, Exposing, & Overcoming Aversions*, the hiring manager should handle aversions throughout the interview process. But you should still have one last meeting before extending a job offer to finalize your agreement with the candidate. Here's why (and here's what I say to the candidate at the start of the Final Aversions Interview): "There are lots of great things we like about you, but we won't focus on those today. We believe there's no perfect candidate and there's no perfect employer. Let's talk about where this *isn't* a perfect match and agree on how each issue should be managed. If we can't agree on a plan to manage an issue, it's better to find out and part ways now rather than after you've been on the job for six months or a year."

In these six intended outcomes of the Final Aversions Interview, you essentially shift from interviewer to manager:

1. <u>To expose candidates to all their aversions</u> and reiterate previously raised aversions that have not been eliminated or resolved. Don't use the Final Aversions Interview as a crutch to avoid exposing aversions throughout the process.

2. <u>To give candidates one more chance to overcome their aversions</u>. If they cannot overcome key aversions, this interview saves you from making a hiring mistake.

3. <u>To give candidates one final chance to present and overcome their aversions</u> about your company.

4. <u>To manage candidates' expectations</u>. Let them know exactly what they are signing up for and what you will expect in order for them to remain employed with your company. At the conclusion of the Final Aversions Interview, you should send candidates away to think about the gravity of the choice they are about to make. If you are introducing important expectations and responsibilities for the first time at this stage, that is a failure of your interview process. You should have managed candidates' expectations at every opportunity. Most of what is discussed in the Final Aversions Interview is presented for emphasis, not as new information.

5. <u>To Set Them Up For Future Reference</u>. As you may recall from previous chapters, STUFFR consists of identifying, understanding, and discussing potential problems and making a note of candidates' (and your) exact words and commitment to not failing. Candidates are rarely eliminated from the hiring process at the Final Aversions Interview unless new data is disclosed or you're given reason to believe their aversions cannot be overcome. You are detailing areas in need of improvement and delivering a clear message that your company will not tolerate below-standard behavior. To have a successful career at your company, candidates must exhibit continuous self-improvement and work within established principles and guidelines.

6. <u>To give an accurate picture of the struggles candidates will face on the job, and emphasize the rewards for hard work</u>. When you push candidates away, you have to provide info that will pull them in slightly stronger.

Common Aversions

The heart of communication during the Final Aversions Interview isn't any different from what was detailed in the chapter on *Uncovering, Exposing, & Overcoming Aversions*, but this is the final shot for both you and the candidate to overcome the aversions. The only mechanical difference between the Final Aversions Interview and other interviews is the time you should devote to discussing what my company calls common aversions. It is a best practice to review these common aversions prior to making a job offer. This will manage candidates' expectations, Set Them Up For Future Reference, and ensure that you've exposed them to every important potential job- and company-related hardship. My company developed this list of common aversions over time, based on failure analyses of past hires. We failed to present this information to some candidates during the interview process and discovered, soon after they joined us, that they were not a fit for our company. We don't want to repeat that mistake, so we wrote them down and integrated them into our pre-employment process.

Review of candidates' pre-employment tests. Explain in detail what the test is telling you about the candidate's mapping and current skill level. Validate the candidate's agreement that the test results are accurate, explain how the candidate's mapping aligns with your target for the position, and discuss how it will be a help or hindrance on the job.

Work hours. Specify what times the workday starts and ends, reiterate the need to be on time, and manage expectations about overtime. Does being on time mean being in the building or actually working by a specific time?

Paid-leave time. Discuss vacation time, personal time, and how to schedule time off.

Travel expectations. Imagine the results of *not* making this clear before you make the job offer: You ask the employee to spend three days at a trade show and two days visiting customers, and they reply, *Sorry, I can't be away from home that long.*

Constructive criticism. Reiterate how much criticism employees will receive and how frequently their performance will be reviewed (daily? weekly? monthly? quarterly? annually?). I recall an editor candidate telling us, "I'm my own worst critic." Knowing the editor's work would be scrutinized by our copy editor, chief editor, managing editor, proofreaders, advertisers, and subscribers, I responded, "After a couple months here, you won't make your own top 10 list."

Pace of job. We let inside sales candidates know how many sales contacts and how much phone time they'll have to produce in a typical day. We let editor candidates know approximately how many pages of editorial they will need to produce each month. Candidates who think our standards are too stringent can choose not to work for us. That rarely happens. The reality is that we Set Them Up For Future Reference when we ask them to meet those productivity goals after they're hired.

No moodiness, rudeness, cursing, or loss of emotional control at work. This very important point should be discussed with every candidate. You'll rarely see a candidate lose emotional control in an interview, so don't skip this discussion just because the problem hasn't presented itself. I'll repeat exactly what I say about this with candidates: "You can take what I'm about to say to you as me wagging my finger in your face saying, 'We have a bunch of good, honest, kind, hard-working people here. Don't screw it up. I'll throw you out of here because I don't want one person ruining it for everybody.' Or you can take what I'm saying as our company making a commitment to you that you don't have to tolerate anyone screaming, yelling, swearing, or belittling you. If someone breaks the Golden Rule, let me know and we'll put a stop to it." If a recently hired employee violates the Golden Rule, the hiring manager can use this conversation to quash the problem as soon as it arises.

<u>Talking long.</u> Candidates tend to be on top of their communication game during interviews. But they could actually be "that guy" — the long-winded employee you avoid in the hallway. We Set Them Up For Future Reference that talking long is unacceptable and will harm their productivity and their co-workers' productivity and job satisfaction. We're not afraid to address that issue during the pre-employment process or during an employee's career with us.

<u>The necessity of attention to detail.</u> We tell sales candidates they don't have to be the world's best at details, but we want all employees to care about details. We believe that small actions performed well every day lead to greatness. We don't have secretaries to clean up after us, to tabulate our reports, or to handle lower-level tasks.

That's *our* list. Use it as a guideline to develop a list of common aversions that apply to your company and to spark mini-conversations that can extinguish future employee complaints. And be sure you don't treat all common aversions as equal. Emphasize those most pertinent to the candidate and the job.

Discussing Pay

No pressure, but don't screw up this part of the conversation. Take pay discussions seriously and come to the table armed with every relevant fact. Spell out all specifics of their pay including base, commission, overtime, and bonuses. We go as far as estimating what a candidate's W-2 could look like after a full year on the job. There should be zero surprises about pay and benefits in an employee's first paycheck.

Manage candidates' expectations of future pay and be prepared to map out a variety of possibilities. Are pay adjustments based on merit, tenure, or promotion? Is there an annual cost-of-living raise? Does the employee have to ask for a raise? While you're managing expectations, use the phrase *as of now*. Let candidates know this pay structure isn't guaranteed for life and that the company reserves the right to change it. To calm candidates' nerves and to show you're not trying to hoodwink them, share details of the last time the pay structure changed and why.

I have very rarely (like once) negotiated pay with a candidate in the Final Aversions Interview. We do the hard thinking and thorough research up front, so we're confident about the number we're offering. If the candidate has data to share that we don't have, I'll look at it. But if you've properly prepared, you should have confidence in your number. If a candidate holds out for higher pay but doesn't have facts to back that demand, treat the insistence like a Last Presented Issue. Address the fact that the candidate's false conclusion is based on feelings, not data. I don't know much about your company, but I'll assume that you want employees who are in the habit of basing decisions on facts, not just feelings.

When the pay discussion seems to have concluded, ask: *How do you feel about this pay? If we made a job offer at this pay, would you accept it?* You shouldn't walk out of the Final Aversions Interview wondering if a candidate will accept your job offer.

Here's the biggest pay-related curveball we've received: Adam, a candidate for a position in the operations side of our business, had stated in a previous interview that he would take our job if we offered a $40,000 annual salary. That was the number we were thinking about and a sizeable raise over his current wage. So when we talked pay at the Final Aversions Interview, we thought Adam would be thrilled to be offered $40,000. At the same time, we let him know we'd be moving in a few months to a bigger office east of our current location. Our relocation would add about 10 minutes to his daily commute. Adam reacted by saying that the pay offer should be $42,000 to cover the extra gas he'd have to use. The extra commuting time might have cost him $100–$200 more over the course of a year; he was clearly trying to wedge us to his advantage. So, following logic, we asked if he'd have asked us to lower our offer to $38,000 if we were moving our office closer to his house. Adam accepted our $40,000 offer.

Send Them Away

We don't make a formal job offer at the Final Aversions Interview, no matter how well the conversation goes. We send candidates away to think about the gravity of the choice they are about to make.

Here's some language I've used at this point: "Well, you've made it this far and, from our perspective, things have gone really well. Now you have to ask yourself a few questions. Are we right for you? Are you ready to sign up for this challenge? We've spent 15 hours with you, which is a long time for an interview process. But we still don't know you anywhere close to as well as you know yourself. You will know better than anyone if taking this job is the best thing for you to do. You are signing up for the rewards, but also committing to make the effort necessary to earn them. Can you do it? Do you *want* to do it? I'm not asking you to answer those questions now. Think about it tonight, and we'll talk tomorrow morning on the phone."

This brief speech sets the stage for managing the candidate. We've already mentioned that we believe the candidate is a good fit and clearly outlined what we expect. Now the candidate is making the choice about living up to our expectations. If a candidate accepts our offer the next day (which always happens) and, as an employee, doesn't live up to what we agreed on during the interview process (which sometimes happens), our notes and our words from the Final Aversions Interview can help get the employee back on track.

Job Offer

The formal job offer is an extension of the Final Aversions Interview. So I'll include details here instead of devoting an entire chapter to what should be a rote, standard process.

The hiring manager typically extends a job offer on the business day after the Final Aversions Interview and should say: "At this point, I am offering you the job. Do you accept?" This constitutes a formal job offer and requires a *yes* or *no* response.

After the candidate accepts, clarify your go-forward plan.

- Specify the start date and time and where and to whom the candidate should report. If the start date is more than one week out from the job offer, establish a schedule for the candidate to call the hiring manager weekly or more often. This affords the candidate an opportunity to ask questions as they arise and continues to build the candidate's enthusiasm for the job. This is also a test of whether the candidate follows directions and can manage an ongoing task. Do actions in this situation match the candidate's words during the interview process?

- Arrange for currently employed candidates to update you, soon after giving their quit notice, on how that went. This provides an emotional outlet for candidates after having this hard conversation. Also, no-nonsense companies sometimes terminate employees the day they give notice, which could change the anticipated start date.

Even though the job offer is straightforward, the conversation should be filled with enthusiasm. It's a special day when you find a person who has the skills, personality, character, and mapping to grow into a great performer for your organization.

PART IV

---

258 Tremendous
Interview Questions

Please use the following pages as a guideline for developing questions for your interviews, but only if you've read the previous three sections of this book. Asking these questions without understanding the *why* behind each one is dangerous. You won't make the right hiring decisions because you won't fully understand the best practice principles or the outcomes you're shooting for. I'm serious, darn it. If you haven't read this entire book, go back to Chapter 1 and start reading.

The questions are divided into eight sections:

1. Phone Screen Questions: My company asks these questions during a 15-minute phone conversation to determine if a 1st Interview is appropriate.

2. Standard 1st Interview Questions: We ask these questions (and appropriate follow-up questions) of pretty much every candidate we bring into our office.

3. Standard 2nd Interview Questions: If a candidate survives the 1st Interview, we ask many of these questions. Prior to this interview, you will want to pick and choose questions and list them in the order you plan to ask them.

4. Final Aversions Interview Questions: The heart of the Final Aversions Interview is questions and comments tailored to the candidate's specific aversions. I've included a general outline for that discussion. You'll have to fill in most of the blanks based on what you've uncovered about the candidate.

5. Questions for Manager and Executive Candidates: Every hire you make is important, but hiring the right managers and senior executives carries even more weight. I consider managers and executives to be in *hub positions* — like the hub is the center of a wheel. Hiring the wrong person for a hub position will negatively impact multiple employees. Hiring and appropriately managing the right person creates a big lift for your entire organization, especially the group that employee directs. Because of the added importance, ask these candidates additional questions to increase your chances of making the right hire. You'll need to add hours to your pre-employment process, but making the right decision justifies the extra time.

6. <u>Questions for Senior Executive Candidates:</u> From time to time, you may have to hire a director, vice president, or general manager who will lead an entire department or division of your company. These positions require special experience and a unique skill set. Interview these people in the office first. Then, if they pass those tests, question them for an entire weekend from as many angles as you can think of. This hire could send your company soaring … or crashing. Because of the long-term ramifications and the pain misfiring causes, ask these questions to paint a complete picture of a candidate's life and career to date.

7. <u>Questions for Sales Candidates:</u> Friendly reminder: Hire for skill, personality, character, and mapping. Don't allow yourself to be hypnotized by a likeable, well-spoken candidate who boasts of past sales success. A common mistake made by hiring managers in the pre-employment process is looking only to answer the question of whether a candidate can sell. The questions in this section focus on sales skills and sales experience, but don't skip over 1st and 2nd Interview questions about character and mapping. HR professionals will tell you that most of their company's rules (and their own gray hair) result from nutty things done by sales reps. Capable salespeople who are successful, fun, and have high character do exist. Hold out to hire them.

8. <u>Questions for Recent College Graduates:</u> In the rare instances when my company hired college graduates, we asked these questions in addition to many of our standard interview questions.

All of these questions have value. But some have given me exceptional insight into candidates. Those questions — call them Jimmy's Favorites — are marked with this symbol: ☺

Phone
Interview Questions

1.   How did you hear about our company and the position you applied for?

2.   Why did you apply?

2a.   What do you find enticing about our company and the position?

3.   Have you ever applied for employment with our company in the past?

3a.   If *yes*, when?

3b.   Did you have an interview?

4.   Are you related to or are you friends with any employees who work at our company now?

5.   What are your long-term goals? What are your plans for:

5a.   Further education?

5b.   Your career?

5c.   Where you want to live?

  ☺ *This question is typically the most insightful of the Phone Interview. At this point, candidates will reveal if their long-term goals match what your company offers.*

6.   Are you willing to relocate if necessary?

  Ask this question only if the candidate does not currently reside in the city where you're hiring.

7.   When are you available for an interview?

To help manage candidates' expectations, explain the approximate number of days and the general purpose of each interview stage in your pre-employment process. One business outcome for doing this is to ensure that the candidate understands the reasonableness of a lengthy, non-traditional interview process. A desired emotional outcome is the candidate not becoming frustrated with your extended interview process.

Standard
1st Interview Questions

Introduction

a.   *Establish rapport; put the candidate at ease. Don't immediately jump into the interview questions. Chat about where the candidate attended school or another interesting résumé item.*

b.   *Emphasize that you want the candidate to answer questions completely and candidly; you <u>don't</u> want standard job interview answers. Explain that you're looking for a match between employee and employer. If this is not a match, that's fine. You don't want to find that it's a mismatch six weeks after the candidate becomes an employee.*

c.   *To help manage expectations, explain your interview process. Let candidates know the purpose of this interview and what subsequent interviews they may participate in.*

d.   *Manage the candidate's expectations about the length of this interview.*

8.   How much time do you have for today's interview?
     This interview should take about an hour — maybe longer, depending on how the questions go.
     ☺*Saying this gives you the opportunity to bail in 60 minutes if the candidate turns out to be an obvious non-hire. You'll still get the emotional outcomes of not rushing the candidate out the door, but you won't waste your entire day talking with someone you know won't be working with you.*

9.   How did you hear about us? What attracted you to us?

Résumé Review

Ask the following questions while reviewing the candidate's résumé. Ask why the candidate left each job. Continue to ask until the candidate runs out of answers. Take complete notes on the résumé.

10.   Have you had any other jobs not listed on your résumé?

10a.   Why didn't you list those jobs on your résumé?

11.   During this interview, I'm going to ask how much you were paid at previous jobs. At some point in our process, we will ask you to verify your answers by bringing in past pay stubs. Would you be OK with that?

12.   Under what type of pay structures have you worked (e.g., base salary only, commissions, incentive/bonus pay, paid overtime)?

13.   How satisfied or dissatisfied were you with this compensation structure? Why?

14.   Tell me about the event/the exact moment that caused each job to come to an end and the conversation that took place.

15.   Describe the pay and benefits you received for each position.

16.   Would your most recent employer hire you back?

17.   Would any of your previous employers *not* hire you back?

17a.   Why?

18.   Would you *not* work for any of your previous employers?

18a.   Why?

19.   In as much detail as possible, tell me why you want to leave your present job.

20.   Does your current employer know you're looking for work?

20a.   If *no*, why not?

21.   Describe a typical day in your current job.

22.   What do you find most fulfilling in your current position? And what do you find most frustrating?

23. Financial: You may be required to travel periodically for our company. You will be required to pay for your travel expenses while you are on the road. These expenses could amount to as much as $_____ during a busy month. Could you cover these expenses with credit cards or cash until you could be reimbursed by the company?
23a. Which method would you use?
The answers No *or* Cash *could be a sign of financial instability and should be listed as an aversion. Any kind of personal or financial instability will likely affect the candidate's work performance.*

24. Where are you now in your job search? Are you actively looking?
24a. If so, what other types of companies and positions have you looked at or applied to?
☺*Candidates will tell you they're certain your job is the exact career they're looking for. But answering this question often divulges that they're open to anything that will pay the bills. I've talked with candidates for a full-time sales position who were spending all their energy applying for clerical or non-professional part-time jobs.*

25. What would you like to be doing in two or three years? And what would you like to be earning by then?
☺*I'm always surprised how quickly this question can help eliminate candidates whose own words tell you that their near-term career path doesn't remotely match up with your company. I recall a candidate who replied that she wanted to be "anywhere but this town. I want to be in a big city." Since our company wasn't planning to leave town and the position couldn't be adapted for a remote employee, her answer basically ended our interview process.*

26. What would you like to be doing in 10 years? What's your career goal in 10 years?

27. If you weren't going to be here in 10 years, what would cause you to leave?
27a. What would cause you to stay?

28. In as much detail as possible, tell me why you would like our job.

29. What is the most difficult thing about your current job? How do you handle it?

30.   What motivates you?

31.   How much overtime have you worked recently?
32.   When did you work most of your overtime: before 8, after 5, or on weekends?
33.   How do you feel about overtime?

34.   How much did you travel in your past jobs?
35.   How do you feel about out-of-town/overnight travel?
36.   Would being on the road _____ times in one month be OK?

37.   What was the dress code at your past jobs? How did you like it?
38.   Explain our dress code. Ask how the candidate feels about our dress code.

39.   What are your thoughts on driving in from out of town every day? Have you made a similar commute before? *(Ask this only if the candidate will have a 25-minute or longer commute to your workplace.)*

40.   What were the work hours like at your most recent job?
41.   How did you like those hours?
42.   Our work hours are _____. How do you feel about that?

43.   Have you ever signed a non-compete agreement?
44.   Would you be OK signing a non-compete agreement with us?

(These next two questions may be illegal in some states where smokers are a protected class.)
45.   Do you smoke?
46.   Everyone who works here signs a no-smoking agreement. Smoking is not permitted on company premises — in the building or on the parking lot — at any time of day or night, including weekends, at lunchtime even if you leave the premises, at any company function anywhere, or at trade shows at any time. Would you sign that no-smoking agreement?

47.   There is a lot of constructive criticism here. How will you feel about that?

48.   Give me an example of a valuable criticism you've received. How did it help you? How did you react to it?

48a.   Thank you. Can you give me another example?

49.   Let's talk about you giving criticism. Give me an example of a time when you had to do the hard thing or have a difficult conversation. Here are some examples: telling someone "no," selling someone on doing things your way, managing someone's expectations.
49a.   Thank you. Can you give me another example?

50.   We work hard here. The pace is fast. Getting your work done on time will not be easy. How do you feel about this?
50a.   How does this compare to your current/previous job?

51.   How does our pre-employment process compare with other companies you know of?

52.   We just have a few minutes left. Is there anything else we should talk about?

53.   If we progress to the point where a job offer is made, what salary range do you expect? Why?
       ☺*Lots of hiring managers wait until the end of their interview process to ask this question. Well, what if the absolute most you could pay for a position was $60,000 and the candidate required $100,000? Better to find that out before you and your staff have spent hours interviewing a candidate your company can't afford.*

54.   We're not through with the interview process yet. But if we offered you this job now, would you take it? If *yes,* on what basis?

I will get together with (the person at the next level of our hiring process) in the next couple days to talk about our next step. We will decide if we would like to continue the process with you or if we want to pursue other candidates for the position. We will call you and let you know what we decide. If you don't hear from us in two days, please give me a call.

End of 1ˢᵗ Interview

Standard
2nd Interview Questions

Introduction

a.　*Establish rapport; put the candidate at ease. Don't immediately jump into the interview questions. Chat about where the candidate went to school or another interesting résumé item.*

b.　*Emphasize that you want the candidate to answer questions completely and candidly; you <u>don't</u> want standard job interview answers. Explain that you're looking for a match between employee and employer. If this is not a match, that's fine. You don't want to find that it's a mismatch six weeks after the candidate becomes an employee.*

c.　*To help manage expectations, explain your interview process. Let candidates know the purpose of this interview and what subsequent interviews they may participate in.*

d.　*Manage the candidate's expectations about the length of this interview.*
How much time do you have for today's interview?
This interview should take about an hour — maybe longer, depending on how the questions go.

55.　Where are you now in your job search? Are you actively looking?

55a.　If so, what other types of companies and positions have you looked at or applied to?

Ask several specific follow-up questions to clarify and validate answers from the 1ˢᵗ Interview. Then introduce your own questions.

56. How would you evaluate the strengths and weaknesses of the company you were with last?

57. How did you feel about that company's policies and procedures? Too many? Too few?

58. Tell me how you felt about your last supervisor in terms of fairness and competence.

59. How did you feel about the caliber of your co-workers?

60. What would your current/previous employer say are your strengths and weaknesses?
    Strengths:
    Weaknesses:

61. Do you agree? If not, what would *you* say are your strengths and weaknesses?

62. Give me an example of changing your behavior for work reasons.

63. What's the last thing on which you and your boss disagreed? How did you settle it?
63a. Thank you. Can you give me another example of a time you and your boss disagreed?

64. Can you give me an example of you exceeding your supervisor's expectations?
64a. Why did you do it?

65. What are your top five accomplishments in life?
    ☺*At this point in your interviews, you should have a pretty good read on whether the candidate has the personality and skills to survive your pre-employment process. But this question and the following one let you know if the candidate has actually accomplished anything career-wise. These are the questions I jump to if I'm sensing the candidate is "light" — presents well but doesn't have much substance. I once asked this question of a young candidate who fit that description. She could come up with only four answers. And #3 was "being named Homecoming Queen in high school."*

66. What are your top five professional accomplishments?

    ☺ *Tying in to what I wrote above, this question hones in on what the candidate has actually done at work. Lots of candidates will answer the previous question with family-related or school-related accomplishments (e.g., raising great kids, being the first in the family to go to college). This question talks work and nothing but work.*

67. What do you consider the single most important idea you contributed or your single most noteworthy accomplishment in your <u>present</u> job?

68. What do you consider the single most important idea you contributed or your single most noteworthy accomplishment in your <u>previous</u> job?

69. Tell me about a time you failed at something and what you learned as a result of that experience.

69a. Thank you. Can you give me another example of a time you failed or fell short?

70. Describe an unpleasant work situation and how you dealt with it.

70a. Thank you. Can you give me another example?

71. Tell me about a problem you've had with someone you encountered on a regular basis. How did you solve it?

71a. Thank you. Can you give me another example?

72. Give me an example of a time when you weren't getting along with a co-worker. How did you resolve that situation?

72a. Thank you. Can you give me another example?

73. Can you tell me about a job experience in which you had to speak up to be sure that other people knew what you thought or felt?

73a. Thank you. Can you give me another example?

74. Give me an example of the last time you had to exercise self-control to protect a relationship.

74a. Thank you. Can you give me another example?

75. Tell me about a time you dealt with an angry or frustrated customer.

75a. Thank you. Can you give me another example?

76. Describe a time that you had to work on a deadline or under pressure. How did you handle it?

76a.   Thank you. Can you give me another example?

77.   Have you ever had to work extra hours or change your personal plans to deal with an emergency at work? Describe the situation and what you did. How often did these occasions arise?

78.   Tell me about a recent split-second decision you made on the job. Why did you make that decision, and how did things turn out?

78a.   Thank you. Can you give me another example?

79.   Give me an example of a problem you faced on any job you have had, and tell me how you solved it.

79a.   Thank you. Can you give me another example?

80.   Give me an example of an important goal you set in the past, and tell me about your success in reaching it.

80a.   Thank you. Can you give me another example?

81.   Tell me about a goal you accomplished at work that you were particularly proud of.

81a.   Thank you. Can you give me another example?

82.   How do you organize yourself for day-to-day activities?

83.   How do you feel about our company's size and industry?

84.   What tasks do you find most stimulating or interesting? What tasks do you like least?
       Most stimulating:
       Least stimulating:

85.   What things are you looking for in a job? What is your ideal job?

86.   Tell me about a time you were recognized for an accomplishment. What did you do that was recognized?

86a.   What kind of recognition did you receive? (monetary, public recognition)

86b.   How did you feel about the reward?

86c.   Would you have preferred a different type of reward? If so, what?

87.   How do you feel about the level of recognition you currently receive?

87a.   Why do you feel that way?

88.   Have you ever owned your own business or do you run a sideline business?

89.   Would you like to someday own your own business? Why or why not?

90.   What do you think it takes for a person to be successful in (position applied for)?

91.   Have you taken any steps to improve your work skills or performance?
91a. Give me examples of actions you've taken.

92.   Are you currently involved in any self-improvement activities that aren't 100% focused on work skills?

93.   What books have had the greatest effect on your life?

94.   What business books have had the greatest effect on your career?

95.   Part of emotional maturity is acquiring self-insight. Give me an example of something you recently learned about yourself.
      ☺*Nobody is ever prepared for this one. The most common answer I get is, "Ummm … hmmm … well …" You'll learn that some people just aren't that deep. They're living and working, but not really learning. They're getting older, but not focusing on getting better. Maybe the best answer I ever heard to this question was from an accountant candidate who said he asked his wife what he does that frustrates her most. She said that whenever something needs to be done, he jumps in and immediately wrestles every detail to the ground. She felt she didn't have control of anything in their marriage because he never let her do anything from start to finish. He explained to her (and to us) that he wasn't a control freak. He just wanted to help his wife, whom he adored. When he got this feedback, he began communicating with her on this subject and struck the right balance of when to help and when to let go. I wanted to hire the guy right then and there for caring so much about his wife and her needs, communicating with her so openly, and changing his behavior so quickly. We eventually hired him, and he's proven to be an excellent employee. And the kind of guy you pray your daughter marries.*

96.   We've asked a lot of hard questions, but this one is the easiest: What would you like to tell me about yourself? What one point did you want to make clear to me in this interview?

97.   The purpose of an interview is for me to find out what is *in* you. So let me just ask: What are you passionate about? What things excite you the most?

98.   We just have a few minutes left. Is there anything else we should talk about?

99.   We're not through with the interview process yet. But if we offered you this job now, would you take it?

99a.   If *yes*, on what basis?

☺*This is a great question to ask at this point, because you'll learn something about the candidate's critical thinking skills. If the candidate says, "Absolutely! I'll accept your offer!" but still hasn't asked you key questions, you will want to drill down on a decision not based on facts.*

I will get together with _____ in the next couple days to talk about our next step. We will decide if we would like to continue in the process with you or if we want to pursue other candidates for the position. We will call you and let you know what we decide. If you don't hear from us in two days, please give me a call.

End of 2ⁿᵈ Interview

Final Aversions
Interview Questions

A. *Establish rapport; put the candidate at ease. Don't immediately jump into the interview questions.*

B. *Manage the candidate's expectations for the interview; explain the purpose of the interview.*

> There are lots of great things we like about you, but we won't focus on those today. We believe there's no perfect candidate and there's no perfect employer. Let's talk about where this *isn't* a perfect match and agree on how each issue should be managed. If we can't agree on something or agree on a plan to manage an issue, it's better we find that out and part ways now, rather than after you've been on the job for six months or a year.
>
> Also, there won't be a job offer today. We'll talk about a lot of things that we want you to think about overnight.

C. *Ask catch-up questions or thoughts.*
100.   How did your spouse/significant other like dinner?
101.   Is he/she eager for you to make this move?

D. *Discuss the candidate's aversions to your company.*
102.   Let's talk about your aversions first. What concerns do you have?
        Prior to asking this question, you should have compiled a list of all concerns the candidate expressed during the previous interviews. If the candidate doesn't bring up those aversions again, ask why. Did the candidate acquire data to overcome the aversions or just forget?

E. *Discuss your aversions of the candidate.*

> *This is the heart of the Final Aversions Interview. Because each candidate's aversions are unique, you'll have to develop the questions and comments for this conversation. Take good notes in order to Set Them Up For Future Reference.*

F. *Discuss pay.*

103. Let's talk pay. I'd encourage you to take detailed notes so you fully understand the numbers and can refer to them later. I'm going to talk long here to spell out every detail so you get the full picture. Ready?

> *Because my company pays overtime, we would talk base salary and bonuses (plus commission for sales candidates), then work up some scenarios for overtime. e.g., "If you worked two hours of overtime a week, your W-2 would end up right around $X. If you worked five hours of overtime each week, your W-2 would be right about $Y."*

104. How do you feel about this pay?

105. What are your thoughts or questions about this pay structure and the amounts?

106. If we offered you the job at this pay, would you accept it?

107. What are the chances your current employer will make a counteroffer that will entice you to stay?

107a. Can you give me an exact percentage of the likelihood that you'd accept their counteroffer?

> ☺*It's very common for employers to freak out when good employees give their quit notice and beg them to stay by offering a pay raise or promotion. But if you ask the "exact percentage" question, you will likely get an answer like, "There's no way I'd accept their offer. There's a 0% chance I'd stay." That's what most people will say in a face-to-face conversation right after you've talked about pay they like. So when the candidate gives their quit notice and gets that whopper of a counteroffer from their current boss, they will have to go back on their assurances to you during this conversation. Most people won't do that. People like to make their word good. You have to first Set Them Up For Future Reference with these questions.*
>
> *If the answer to the "exact percentage" question isn't a loud and clear 0% chance of accepting the counteroffer, you've got a brand new — and major — aversion to discuss.*

108.   Why would you take your current employer's offer to stay?

109.   Why wouldn't you want our job?

110.   We talked about how you wanted to leave your job because of ____, ____, and ____. Can you talk about why money would now make the difference?

G. *Common aversions*

Take a look at my company's list, then develop a list of common aversions that apply to your company. Don't treat all common aversions as equal. Emphasize those which most apply to the candidate and the job.

• Review the pre-employment tests with the candidate.

• Discuss work hours.

• Reiterate the amount of paid-leave time.

• Outline travel expectations for the job.

• Explain the importance of constructive criticism.

• Describe the pace of the job.

• Emphasize that moodiness, rudeness, cursing, or loss of emotional control at work is unacceptable.

• Remind the candidate that talking long is harmful.

• Emphasize that attention to detail is necessary to succeed.

H. *Potential start date*

111.   If we offered you this position and you accepted, what date would you expect to start?

I. *Clarify when you'll talk with the candidate next.*

112.   Like I said in the beginning, we talked about a lot of things today that we want you to think about overnight. What would be a good time for me to call you tomorrow?

Questions For
Manager Candidates

Leadership:

113.   Do you consider your previous/current company successful?

113a. If *yes,* why? What was the company's formula for success?

113b. If *no,* why not?

114.   Did you personally ever make moves to change the markets your company served or the industries it operated in? How did your suggestions/changes work out?

115.   Can you tell me a couple of examples of systems or processes you installed that didn't exist in the company before you worked there?

115a. How did you ensure those systems didn't erode? How did you make sure they operated successfully for years?

116.   Can you tell me about a decision that you alone initiated that improved profitability?

117.   Improved product quality or customer service?

118.   Improved productivity?

119.   Tell me about a system you initiated that increased productivity among multiple co-workers — either company-wide or department-wide.

120.   Tell me about a time you identified a problem and took action to correct it rather than wait for someone else to do it.

121. Tell me about a recent decision you made that displayed integrity or high character.
121a. Thank you. Can you give me another example?

122. Talk about the kinds of deadlines you've struggled with in a prior job or in your current job.

123. Did you make any adjustments to ensure you achieved all your deadlines? To what degree were those adjustments successful?

124. Did you ever have an employee who struggled to achieve deadlines? How did you resolve that situation?

Interaction With Direct Reports:

125. How many employees were you directly responsible for at your current/previous job?
126. How many of these employees were below standard?
127. For each employee, how did you react?

128. Tell me about a time you had an employee who wasn't hitting the performance standard: Where the standard was <u>work quality</u>. How did you resolve it?

129. Where the standard was <u>work quantity</u>. How did you resolve it?

130. Where the standard was <u>good attitude</u>. How did you resolve it?

131. Can you tell me about the last time you had to tell an employee that they had to improve their performance or else they would be let go?

132. Tell me about the hardest conversation you ever had with an employee.

Interaction With People Other Than Direct Reports:

133. Have you ever felt the need to apologize to a co-worker?
133a. If *no:* Looking back, can you think of a time when you should have apologized but didn't?
133b. If *yes*, what was the occasion? Can you give me some details about that?
133c. Thank you. Can you give me another example?

134. What skills/qualities contribute to building productive relationships with co-workers?

135. Give me an example of when you've used these skills with a specific co-worker.

136. Give me an example of when you did not use these skills/qualities and fell short of your outcome.

137. Describe your relationship with the owners/executive management at your present company.

138. Can you tell me about a time you had to confront a supplier about aligning with your company's goals?
138a. Thank you. Can you give me another example?

139. Tell me about a time when you received a product or service from a vendor that was less than what you expected.
139a. How did you handle the situation?

140. How do you monitor your customers' satisfaction? Give me some specific details and examples.

141. Can you tell me about a time you had to confront a customer about getting in line with your company's goals?
141a. Thank you. Can you give me another example?

142. At your last job, how often did you have to make outbound calls to customers, vendors, or other constituents who were upset with your company, or to forewarn them that you weren't going to meet their expectations?
142a. What were some examples?

Problem-Solving & Project Management:

143. Can you give me an example of a time when you had to solve a really complex problem that required multiple steps across weeks or months?

144. There's a difference between a manager working *in the business* vs. working *on the business.* Can you give me examples from your previous/current jobs of times where you, as a manager, worked in the business and times where you worked on the business?

145. Did your previous companies have policy and procedure manuals?
145a. What subjects did they cover?
145b. Were they used?
145c. Did you find them valuable? Why or why not?
145d. Were you able to keep them updated? Why or why not?

146. Walk me through a situation in which you asked numerous questions of several people to get the information you needed to make an effective decision.
146a. How did you know what to ask?

147. Tell me about a time you accomplished something at work that required you to "rally from behind" — when the project was off track and you had to scramble to get the outcome. What did you do to achieve the outcome?

148. Many obstacles can prevent an organization from achieving goals. Tell me about a time when you met such an obstacle. What did you do to overcome this challenge?

149. Tell me about the hardest conversation you ever had with a co-worker who wasn't following the guidelines for a project you were managing.

150. Describe one strong example of how you managed and tracked a multiperson, multidepartment project.

151. Give an example of a time when multiple people had conflicting opinions or ideas on the project. How did you handle it?

152. Tell me about a time when your standard approach to problem-solving didn't produce the desired solution. What did you do?

153. Tell me about a time when you worked long and hard on a project/report, believed you had completed your work, and your supervisor returned it to you for additional work. Describe the project and the steps you needed to take to complete it.
153a. What was your reaction to having your work handed back for even more work?

154. Tell me about an important project you were working on that had an unreasonable deadline. How did it affect you?
154a. How did you react?

Criticism/Hardiness:

155. What would you identify as personal shortcomings or things you have difficulty doing?

156. How do they affect your ability to perform your job?

157. Have you discussed these shortcomings with anyone? Who? In what setting?

158. What have you done to overcome your shortcomings?

159. What types of criticism have you received from previous supervisors or on past performance reviews?

160. What steps have you taken to change or improve in these areas?

161. Have you ever sought out criticism from your supervisor? How did it go?

162. Have you ever sought out criticism from your direct reports? How did it go?

163. Think about a time you received bad news. What was the news, and what did you do with the information?
163a. How else did you react?

164. Give me an example of a time when you had to adapt to:
164a. A person whose personality was significantly different from yours.
164b. An uncomfortable situation.
164c. An unfamiliar environment.
164d. What did you do to adapt? Why?

165. Tell me about a time you had to work at a fast pace for a long period of time. What kind of work did you do? What did you do to maintain that pace?

166. How stressful was your last job/current job?

167. Which of your former jobs was the most stressful and why?
167a. How did you react?

168.   What was the worst company culture you worked in?
168a. Give me an example of that culture.
168b. How did you cope?

Hiring, Training, & Firing Employees:

169.   Tell me about your philosophy or style of managing employees and the experiences you've had over the years that contributed to your beliefs.

170.   Tell me about the last employee you fired. What led up to it, and how did you do the firing?

171.   Have you personally conducted interviews and made hiring decisions?
171a. If *yes*, tell me what you've learned about that over the years.

172.   With hiring, tell me about the traits you insist on in a candidate worthy of a job offer.

173.   What was your pre-employment process?

174.   What was your biggest hiring mistake? What did you learn from that experience?

175.   Have you read *Hire Like You Just Beat Cancer*? You should. It's a tremendous book. And the author is incredibly handsome.
☺*OK, that last question wasn't real. Here's a new #175 for you:*

175.   What was your employee turnover rate? Why did most people leave?

176.   How did you train new employees?

177.   Did you establish any training programs?

178.   Describe what you've done to link organizational objectives to your direct reports' objectives.

179.   People often feel threatened by change. Tell me about a specific situation and the actions you took to smooth the process of change for others.
179a. Which actions were most successful? Which didn't work?

180. Describe a time when organizational change caused a problem for your group or department. What actions did you take? What was the outcome?

181. Give me an example of a time when multiple people on your team had conflicting opinions or ideas and how you overcame that disagreement.

Growing Sales:

182. Tell me what you did to increase sales at your company.

183. What could you have done to increase sales more?

184. Numerically, what was your sales growth?

185. Was there a sales-growth ceiling?

186. Were you required to follow a specific rate structure or able to "free-lance" rates?

186a. How did you feel about that?

Profitability:

187. Describe your company's profitability.

188. What could you have done to improve it?

189. How often did you look at your company's profitability statements?

190. What types of statements did you look at?

Expenses:

191. What expense-reducing actions did you take to improve profitability?

192. Which expenses were most controllable?

193. What is your philosophy on payroll as an expense?

194. Did you aim to be low-, average-, or high-pay with your employees?

Organizational Skills:

195. Can you give me an example of how you made sure that deadlines and quality standards were met for work that you delegated?

196. Tell me about your time-management system for accomplishing multiple long-term goals and organizing multiple activities. How effective is the system?
196a. Have you made adjustments to your system? If so, what adjustments did you make and why?

197. When scheduling your time, how do you determine priorities?
197a. Can you give me an example of doing that?

Critical Thinking:

198. Between now and our next interview, produce a one-year plan to increase sales and improve profitability for our company.

199. *Give the candidate a copy of your company's guiding principles.* Between now and our next interview, review these documents and come back with questions and comments about our principles.

200. *Give the candidate a copy of the list of qualities and skills your company's managers require.* Between now and our next interview, review this document, develop questions about these qualities, and note which traits are your strongest and weakest.

Questions For
Sr. Executive Candidates

201.   If you were given $1 million to start a company:

201a.   What kind of business would you start? Why?

201b.   What positions would you fill first? Why?

201c.   What steps would you take to get the business profitable in the first or second year?

202.   We sometimes comply with a team decision even though we have personal reservations. Describe a time this happened to you. What did you do?

203.   Think of a time you had a major role in developing a team or project that became very successful. Tell me one or two things you did that ensured the team's success.

204.   Tell me about a time when your actions or words played a critical part in employees realizing your organization's vision.

204a.   What actions did you take to support the vision? What initiatives did you drive to support that vision?

205.   What have you done to ensure that your team understands your company's mission?

206.   Give an example of something you accomplished that others around you said couldn't be done and how you got it done.

207.   Tell me about a department or division that ran efficiently and effectively without much intervention from you. What did you do to get that department/division to the point of self-governance?

208.   The last time you advanced in or left a company, how did your department perform after you left?

209.   What have you done to ensure that direct reports and others in your organization have adequate resources to achieve company goals?

210.   Have you ever helped a peer develop an idea into a successful project or venture? Tell me about your involvement in the development phase and beyond.

211.   There are often people in an organization who deserve more credit than they receive. Tell me about a time when you experienced this. What did you do?

212.   Describe a situation in which you had to decide whether to accept or reject a recommendation. What did you decide? Why?

213.   Can you give me an example of a decision you made that significantly altered company or department policy? Describe your decision-making process.

213a. Thank you. Can you give me another example?

214.   What are the top three lessons you've learned in your professional life?

215.   Not everyone agrees with a manager's decisions. Tell me about an unpopular decision you made and how you gained acceptance from others.

216.   We need information and contributions from others to be effective in our jobs. Describe what you've done to ensure others' participation in a project or idea that was important to you.

217.   Which of your jobs provided you with the opportunity to interact with the widest variety of personalities? How did you manage relationships within that environment?

Questions For
Sales Candidates

218. Tell me about your sales process at your current/previous job.

219. What do you consider a good day's sales effort?

220. What is your understanding of the job you're applying for? What would you be doing every day?

221. Of all your work in sales, have you been more successful servicing clients or developing a new territory? Why?

222. Tell me about a time when you missed your sales goal.
222a. Why did you miss it?
222b. What could you have done differently?
222c. Thank you. Can you give me another example?

223. Do you ever take work home with you? How often?

224. Do you ever work through lunch? How often?

225. Many times, 40 hours a week isn't enough to get everything done here. All our reps work overtime. Some regularly take work home, and some work through lunch. How do you feel about that?

226. What do you think of the work structure and pace we've talked about? What potential problems do you see?

227. Have you worked in the kind of environment we've been discussing? Where?

228. Could you see yourself enjoying this job for 10 years or more? Why?

229. Our reps build relationships, then close the sale. Reps who don't close don't work here. What is your closing rate at your current job?
229a. At previous sales jobs?

230. Give me at least one example of you closing a sale quickly.
230a. Thank you. Can you give me another example?

231. Give me an example of a long sales cycle and your persistence to see the process through to the close.
231a. Thank you. Can you give me another example?

232. What makes you successful or unsuccessful at closing?

233. How much time do you spend on the telephone in your job, and how much time do you spend on the road?
233a. Which do you prefer? Why?

234. What special skills and techniques do you think are required to successfully sell over the phone?

235. What special skills and techniques do you think are required to successfully sell face to face?

236. What kind of roadblocks do you expect from clerical staff? How do you handle them?

237. How many sales calls do you make in a day?
237a. We require __ contacts with a decision maker per day. How do you feel about that?

238. How often do you prepare sales reports? How detailed are they?
238a. We require these sales reports: _____. How do you feel about that?

239. What do you feel are the major personal characteristics of a successful salesperson?

Questions For
Recent College Graduates

240. Why did you choose _____ (name of college)?

241. Why did you choose _____ as your major?

242. Did you ever change majors? Why?

243. Which classes did you find most interesting? Why?

244. What subject gave you the most trouble? Why?

245. Did you participate in any extracurricular activities?

246. Did you lead or organize any extracurricular activities?

247. Did you work part time or during the summer to earn spending money or to help pay expenses?

248. How much time did you spend studying?

249. How early were your classes?

250. How was your class attendance?

251. How were your grades?

252.   Did your grade-point average improve, decrease, or stay the same from year to year?

253.   If you were to start your education over, what would you do differently?

254.   What did you gain from the college experience?

255.   How would your teachers describe you?
255a.   How would your fellow students describe you?
255b.   How would your advisor describe you?

256.   How does this job fit into your overall career plan?

257.   This will be your first job. Why should I believe this will be your last job, too? What data can you give me that in a few years you won't change career plans or want to change employers?

258.   What is the hardest thing you've ever had to do?
258a.   What is the second hardest thing you've ever had to do?

Final Words

Throughout *Hire Like You Just Beat Cancer*, you've read details of lessons I learned about the importance of people decisions. I have one more related anecdote to share with you.

Our copy editor position at Jameson Publishing had been vacant for so long, we were wondering if we'd ever find the right person to fill the role. The owner and I had even gone as far as considering restructuring the department to function without this position. Fortunately for us, Barbara applied for the job. She was moving back to town after working for the United States Patent and Trademark Office in Washington, D.C. I was impressed that she was personable and could also tolerate locking herself in an office to read and research for days if necessary. After she joined our team, she quickly upgraded our editorial best practices and assisted our company's owners during the due diligence phase of a major acquisition.

Coincidentally, Barbara's mother was a nurse manager for a local gastroenterology practice. So when I began having gastrointestinal issues, I asked Barbara for advice on where to turn. She and her mom steered me to the right tests and competent doctors so I could receive the correct diagnosis and treatment. Actually, Barb's mom helped perform my first colonoscopy and called me afterward to confirm that the mass in my colon was cancerous.

Barbara covered for me at work during my recovery from surgery and during chemotherapy. She picked up some of my editorial responsibilities — and occasionally woke me at my desk when the meds got the best of me. As we got to know each other better outside of work, we fell in love. A year later, Barbara and I married, then had a baby daughter and built a new house together. When people ask how Barb and I met, I tell them that our first "date" was her job interview with me way back when.

Best hire I ever made.

Next Steps

Now that you've read *Hire Like You Just Beat Cancer*, I hope you're motivated to do whatever it takes to hire well for your organization. If you'd like to talk about recruiting, interviewing, or hiring, please email me at Jim.Roddy@JamesonPublishing.com. Use "Let's Talk Hiring" as the subject line, and we can set up a time to chat. Or reach out to me through the *Hire Like You Just Beat Cancer* Facebook page, or connect with me on Twitter via @Jim_Roddy. We'll swap stories, and you may ask me as many questions as you wish.

If one conversation doesn't provide all the answers you need, I can steer you toward additional guidance. My company realizes that many organizations like ours suffer under the weight of less-than-best-practice hiring. So we established a sister company called Howland Peterson Consulting to help businesses implement the complete *Hire Like You Just Beat Cancer* system. For more information, send me an email with "Howland Peterson" as the subject line, and I'll connect you with a team of professionals who can help.

Happy hiring!

About the Author

Since 1999, Jim Roddy has educated business leaders through national magazine articles, online columns, webinars, podcasts, video interviews, and presentations at national conferences. Jim joined Jameson Publishing in 1998 as the managing editor for *Business Solutions Magazine*. He was elevated to operations manager in 2002 and then to president/general manager in 2006. Prior to working at Jameson, he was a small-business owner in northwestern Pennsylvania.

His articles and presentations strive to be "infotaining" — a combination of informational and entertaining. Jim is regularly requested to moderate keynote panel discussions featuring executives from companies such as HP, NCR, and IBM.

Jameson Publishing has been named one of the Best Publishing Companies To Work For In The United States by Publishing Executive magazine. Jameson is the only publishing company in the nation to rank in the top 7 of Publishing Executive's list for consecutive years.

Jim is a graduate of Gannon University in Erie, Pennsylvania, where he was a member of the men's basketball team for four years and sports editor of the student newspaper for three years. Jim resides in Erie with his wife, Barbara, and daughter, Evelyn.

A portion of the proceeds from sales of
Hire Like You Just Beat Cancer will be donated to:

The Kanzius Cancer Research Foundation
(www.KanziusCancerResearch.com)
and
The American Cancer Society through Coaches vs. Cancer
(www.cancer.org.)

To order more copies of this book, go to:
www.HireLikeYouJustBeatCancer.com

CPSIA information can be obtained at www.ICGtesting.com
Printed in the USA
LVOW082130101012

302396LV00002B/86/P